The Artist as an Old Man (Self-Portrait)

By
Robert Philip Bolton

Also by Robert Philip Bolton
It's What Eddie Did
The Fable of Flitcroft Point
Jacko. One Bloke. One Year.
*The Boys and Men of Auckland's Mickey Rooney
Gang*
The Fine Art of Kindness
Six Murders?
To The White Gate
Underneath The Arclight
My Marian Year
The Boltons of The Little Boltons
The Tapu Garden of Eden
*For Viktor. The story of Mussorgsky's 'Pictures at an
Exhibition'*
The Collected Short Stories
(in which is combined *Nana's Special Day and other
stories, The Dolphin and other stories,* and *Quickies.)*

Robert Philip Bolton was born in New Zealand in
1945. He has been writing fiction most of his adult
life. Most of his work is about New Zealand and New
Zealanders. He lives in Auckland.

The Artist
as an Old Man
(Self-Portrait)

Copyright © Robert Philip Bolton
ISBN: 978-0-473-72732-1 (Kindle)
ISBN: 978-0-473-72731-4 (paperback)
Cover photo and design by the author

Publisher's note: This book is a transcription of the last entry in the artist's handwritten journal. It has been lightly edited to eliminate unnecessary expletives, expand his abbreviations, amend his sometimes eccentric syntax, and correct spelling and gross grammatical errors. Publishing conventions have also been applied, all to improve the document's readability.

1.

WELL, THAT'S THAT. Home at last after a day that began with boredom and idleness, filling in time for a while, before getting the news from Willy — or at least from Lynley — and wishing I could simply move to Saint Clair there and then and so say goodbye forever to bloody Gregan but thinking — then — that I couldn't because of Uncle Frank.

What a day. Hours and hours of thinking thoughts that were mostly confusing, gloomy and depressing; not at all happy or good. I couldn't help it. And then, later, a climax of sorts with that awful Lallemand character, and his lovely but harassed wife — I can't forget the look on her face — which finally resolved all my doubts about Number Twelve.

And then, sadly but somehow gladly, learning just an hour ago that I really *can* have a fresh start thanks at last to poor old Uncle Frank.

Home now. Ten o'clock on Friday night. Only a couple of hundred metres from the noisy and busy bars, cafés, restaurants and traffic of Ponsonby Road, yet so very quiet. Jaws, asleep in the armchair — what's more homely than a sleeping, heavily-breathing cat? — and me, sitting in my dark kitchen, at my little table and desk-light, a one-bar heater on the floor between me and Jaws, with a mug of hot tea, a goodnight smoke, and this journal.

I started writing it when I decided to leave London, after Fiona. I kept it up to date, with all the unpleasant stuff, through everything, right up to getting on the plane at Heathrow. I brought it with me but until now I haven't opened it since I began The Twelve, a whole year ago. Don't know why. Must have been some sort of therapy then — a way of coping — but this year I've been too busy; perhaps the therapy worked. But now, after tonight, it seems right to bring it up to date, to get all of today — the past year in fact — off my chest and onto paper.

I like paper and hand-writing. I've got a good script — thanks to King's — which anyone who might read this in the future will see for themselves. And, although I like my phone, I've never had a real computer. Wouldn't know where to start. Anyway, Fiona was always there if I needed to look up something, or send or receive an email, anything like that. Acted as my manager, I suppose, which was just as well.

She used her computer all the time. Loved Facebook, although most of what she put there was about me. Said I was famous and that people *wanted* to know. They *deserve* to know, she said. And for posterity. I didn't care. Still don't, really.

Zelnick said Mrs Barkstone found the Facebook page. She said it was all old stuff and well out of date. I suppose Fiona couldn't keep updating it once she got ill. But she — Mrs Barkstone — said my Wikipedia page was pretty detailed and included Fiona right up till the end. I'm sure Fiona didn't do that — couldn't have — but I've got no idea who did.

Well, however and whatever, it's all there — up in the cloud or cyberspace or whatever it's called — all about me, if anyone wants to look. But computer-wise I just never bothered. There's nothing I want or need to look up. These days I get my news mostly from the National programme or *Stuff.* And if someone really wants or needs to contact me they'll find a way. So far they haven't.

So much for my 'fame'.

Anyway, the main thing about today is that it worked. After nearly twenty years away, and this past year-and-a-bit of anonymity, I now know that I really can have a fresh start. I'm now free to head off to faraway Saint Clair to be alone with my thoughts and memories. Meanwhile I've had the time and privacy here, alone, to get The Twelve done without being disturbed.

That would never have happened in London.

Plus, despite that awful Lallemand character, and poor old Uncle Frank, tonight really *was* a success, which pleased Zelnick who has promised to represent me here in Auckland where all the galleries, collectors and buyers are. Meanwhile, no one in London or New York or anywhere else knows where I am, or cares, I suppose. That would have hurt my fragile ego once but not any more. And here — in New Zealand — well, no place on Earth could be farther from the expensive and arty pretentiousness of Chetwin-Lewis's King's Road gallery. And no one I run into here during the day knows anything about me except my name which means nothing to them anyway.

And they don't know anything at all about Fiona.

Which reminds me: the Gallachers knew I was heading back to New Zealand but they don't have an address or anything so I suppose I'll never hear from them again. A bit sad but what can I do?

Zelnick knows everything, of course. So does Mrs Barkstone who tends to 'mother' me with just the right amount of kindness and sympathy.

Zelnick promised to say nothing. I think he liked the intrigue as well, being in on the surprise, the experiment, tonight. In fact, tonight was such a success that he's really happy to be my sole agent once I move to Saint Clair.

I got in touch with them both — Zelnick and Mrs Barkstone — as soon as I got back. Told them the whole story. They remembered me, and knew my London reputation as Julius, but didn't know about Fiona. They promised never to talk about her again, a promise they've kept.

Also, Zelnick knew the value of surprise, so he told no one I was here until he sent out his opening invitation. Those VIPs who received it then were the first to know that I was back, but as Tooks not Julius. And now, after tonight, perhaps the world will know, if it cares, which I doubt. But Zelnick is happy. He knows that keeping the secret was worth it.

I've left him to deal with the publicity. He'll enjoy that; the old bugger loves the limelight.

Willy and Gregan knew, of course, but Willy has naturally (and professionally) kept quiet all this time, while Gregan is too self-centred and selfish to care about anything but himself, his money and his *alleged* cancer.

Tonight's unpleasant encounter with that sad Lallemand man was unfortunate. Everyone saw it, the critics and journos, too, I suppose. His poor wife — such a nice, gentle, sensitive young woman — was so embarrassed. Actually, I feel sorry for him. That sort of attitude. And I do pity his wife. How long will that marriage last?

However, the angry encounter reassured me, accidentally, that I really *can* have a fresh start; the new me. I didn't care then what Lallemand thought or said, and I still don't. I'd never heard of him until tonight and obviously he'd never heard of me, old or new, which was good. His aggressive if somewhat stupid honesty reinforced the fact that London was behind me and that although some people knew of me — although evidently not Mr Lallemand — my reputation has obviously been heavily diluted by time, distance and a minor change of name.

Tonight I was mostly judged on the evidence of my work according to local standards. That was good.

Anyway, it's over now and I'm tired. Despite poor old Uncle Frank, it's a pleasant tiredness; authentic. The sort of tiredness that comes with the satisfaction of a job well done. The sort of tiredness that guarantees a good, healthful and restorative sleep. It's an unbelievably new and refreshing feeling. I'm sure Uncle Frank wouldn't begrudge me that, or a good sleep.

I know that other sort of tiredness well enough: the nervous fatigue that follows 'success'. I had years of it. Despite Fiona's protests, Willoughby and I would celebrate with too much brandy as we, together, counted the cheques and read the reviews.

More wealth and fame.

Driven by greed — for recognition as much as money — after so many years of struggle at home, I debased myself, my talent and my art. That's what Fiona said, and I admit it. She kind of despised me for that. Another young Chetwin-Lewis protégé. That's what she thought at first. Right at the beginning when Willoughby 'discovered' me. She told me so. Eventually she forgave me, for that and much else, thank God. And helped me. Thank God for that, too. Only he knows where I'd be without her.

And now I *am* without her. Forever. And I *hate* it. I'd do anything—

Tonight, though, was my fresh start. On my own, alone, no guiding, encouraging Fiona, into the future. Who knows what that will bring? Old age, I mean. Loneliness? Illness? Nuttiness? Forgetfulness? Full-blown dementia? I'm a bit of all those now. But, whatever happens, starting tomorrow, goodbye, Auckland, hello, Dunedin and my little Bedford Street cottage in Saint Clair.

London, and the world, can continue to wonder whatever the hell happened to Julius Messenger.

I better feed Jaws who's woken up and is pressing hard against my leg, curling his tail around my calf and the chair leg, mewing softly, and looking up at me from the dark below, the warm-red glow of the heater to his side, pleadingly, slow-blinking, as I sit here, smoking, drinking tea, thinking and writing.

It's been a long day for you too, mate, hasn't it. So, to end the day: a late-night packet of Whiskas for you and another smoke for me.

2.

ACTUALLY, THAT'S HOW the day started: feeding Jaws and my first smoke.

Seven o'clock. So early. Yet I was up. A restless, sleepless night. Anticipation, I suppose. At my age, after so many years, I still get nervous. Anyway, up early, ready to go. The usual, necessary and thankfully-regular bodily functions performed. Showered and dressed but not shaved. I haven't been clean-shaven since London — part of the plan, the new and different me — but I've trimmed it myself, roughly, the wiry, greying beard as well as the long and somewhat wild, wavy and greying hair, on occasions. And, I had to admit this morning, an occasion was due. So I planned to see Davy later in the day for a professional tidy-up.

Davy is Dave Wickham. A traditional barber I found up by Richmond Road. He's young but he's an old-fashioned barber, no question. Not a 'Gentleman's Hairdresser' or 'Tonsorial Artiste' but a barber. He's got the red, white and blue striped pole at his door, and red, white and blue stripes around his window. A nice, hard-working young guy — a proper bloody barber — with his own business. I like that.

I knew he'd get me looking presentable, and he did.

Even so, I suppose I still look like a hairy old tramp to some people. Actually, Fiona wouldn't recognize the new me. And Willoughby, who insisted that I should always be clean-shaven, well-groomed and expensively dressed, would be horrified.

Good.

In fact, I've come to not care any more how I look but I knew what Mrs Barkstone wanted. Zelnick, too, I suppose.

You must look presentable, Tooks, she said. There might be photographers and television. (There weren't.)

I got a text from Willy last night saying he wanted to see me this morning. A bit after nine, he said. I thought then — last night, pessimistically — that it was probably a routine thing: he's been keeping me up to date but it's been a long, slow process. I must admit, though, that when I thought about it this morning I hoped it would be about the money at last. Unfortunately, I've thought that before and been disappointed. But this morning *was* different; it *was* about the money.

I didn't know that then, though, not this morning when I got up.

A restless night last night, and an empty day ahead, meant I was up early and bored hardly before the day had begun. Apart from not usually being up that early, I've had months and months of mental and physical busyness here, and an awful couple of years in London before that.

I didn't have breakfast, mainly because I've been too busy to properly shop, getting everything ready, working with Zelnick and Mrs Barkstone. So finally, this morning, with absolutely nothing to do, I thought I might as well go and do it somewhere more interesting than this little flat-cum-studio I share with the inherited Jaws. Coffee and a smoke and, maybe, I thought, if I'm lucky, something to eat.

I checked my wallet. A few dollars and some coins. Enough to buy a coffee. I knew I'd be needing cash during the day — a new packet of tobacco to start with — so I planned to go to the bank later.

It's April. Autumn in New Zealand. They say it's getting chilly but even after one whole winter here last year I still think Auckland's pretty warm. After twenty years in London — New York and Paris too — I know what winter cold is.

So, clean jeans, a favourite but old T-shirt, comfortable old sneakers, and I was ready to go. I pocketed my tobacco and papers, cowboy-boot lighter (a souvenir from Las Vegas), wallet, keys and phone, and then tripped over Jaws as I got to the door.

That gave me a hell of a fright — scared the poor little guy, too — and once would have made me curse with anger but I'm never angry any more. And, anyway, I'm fond of the neutered, always-hungry and somewhat ill-tempered old tabby who came with the flat. So I was a bit delayed as I emptied a packet of Whiskas into his empty and not-very-clean saucer.

Forgot again, mate. Sorry. But there you go. Back soon, eh.

Despite the early hour — early for me — it was already sunny and warm outside. I wouldn't have known, couldn't have known, how sunny and how warm if I'd stayed here in the kitchen, which is not only south-facing but also only a few metres distant from the high brick wall of a nineteenth century saddlery, which is now a trendy house lived in by trendy Ponsonby-type people with trendy furniture, trendy art, and a trendy golden retriever, who always ignore me — the people, not the dog. The dog, whose name I know is Gordon, barks at me in a friendly tone. He did it tonight, when I got home, late, which probably annoyed the trendy but unfriendly neighbours.

They're all right, really. Just a bit snobby for some reason. Perhaps it's the way I look, or the state of Gregan's flats.

They've got such awful art, though. I saw it once. They invited me in. For coffee. To be neighbourly, they said. To show me their small collection. I wondered then — cautiously — if they'd recognized me but they obviously hadn't; they were just pleased with themselves and pleased to have someone to show off to. I tried but couldn't manage to fake enthusiasm for their stuff. Non-committal was the best I could do. I felt bad later. Wished I could apologize. But they haven't spoken to me since.

I like Gordon, though. Pets can't be blamed for the behaviour of their owners, although the reverse isn't true.

The fine weather surprised me this morning only because the studio door's been closed for a week. Still is, even now. It's north-facing, the studio, with big sash windows — sunny and warm and light and welcoming — but I'd shut the door when I left to deliver Number Twelve and I haven't been in there since. That was three days ago. It's probably an awful bloody mess. I know for sure there's a big slice of uneaten pizza on the work table. I should go in and clean up — closure and that — but I don't like the word 'should'. Never have. However, now that everything's settled, now that it's all over with Uncle Frank, now that I don't need Gregan's flat — I'll have to tell him on the weekend —now that I know I'll be moving, I'll have to go in and tidy up.

I'll start on the weekend. Tomorrow.

Now, though, sitting in the dark with my desk light and little heater, and Jaws back to sleep in the armchair, I really don't care.

It's been a long day, a late night, but it's still the Friday after Easter. I knew Zelnick had timed it so his punters would be back from their Sunshine Coast, Gold Coast, Fiji, New Caledonia, Queenstown, Ōmaha, Whangamatā, Pauanui, Taupō, The Mount, Lang's Beach, Mangawhai Heads, etcetera holidays. I guessed that he and Mrs Barkstone were probably busy already — they'd be busy all day — but not me. There was nothing more for me to do until tonight.

It was just a short walk up Jervois Road to Three Lamps. As I said, it was nice, warm and sunny. There were lots of people about. Walking. Waiting at bus stops, frowningly studying something of vital importance on their phones. Lots of traffic, too. Buses. Taxis. Couriers. Ubers. Quite a few electric scooters on the footpath.

Those scootering office girls amaze me. Standing up straight on high heels, staring ahead like zombies, their hair flying in the breeze, little packs on their narrow backs, weaving their way dangerously through the parade of nervous pedestrians. Or on the road.

Same in London. In fact, those scooters — and the new double-decker buses — are about the only things about Ponsonby that have changed since I was here last. That was twelve years ago, for Father's funeral.

I must be getting old and grumpy — actually I *am* getting old and grumpy — but too bad. I think those scooters are really stupid. No registration. No insurance. No licence or crash helmet. And dangerous. Dangerous to their innocent young riders who have no idea how quickly, easily and painfully skin peels off against hard and gritty surfaces; no idea of the fragility of their little manicured fingers, arm bones, leg bones, hip bones, knee bones and head bones. How quickly, easily, and painfully a pretty, made-up face can be ripped and disfigured for life.

And they're dangerous to pedestrians, too — like me — who once had the right of way on the so-called *foot*path.

3.

I WAS SURPRISED how busy it was at Van Goff's. I've never been there early morning before. There was no room inside but it didn't matter; I wanted to sit outside where I could smoke in peace. The few other people sitting outside avoided eye contact — avoided me as usual — although my hairy unkemptness was nothing compared to the sad, dull-eyed druggies and manky homeless who always try to cadge off the outdoor patrons until Van comes out and chases them away. But evidently he wasn't there this morning so we — the other outsiders and I — were vulnerable.

I sat down alone, at a table for two, after putting down my thinning tobacco pack, papers and lighter. Nora was there almost immediately with my long black, a spoon and two brown paper tubes of sugar.

You're early, Tooks, she said.

Everyone seems to know my name — at least my first name — but none seems to have made any connection to the Julius me or, if they have, they haven't said anything. Perhaps they don't care — everyone is the very centre of his own little world — which has suited me fine. And anyway, I've always found that if you go to a shop, café, restaurant, anywhere, more than three times, anywhere in the world, you're considered a regular with a name.

Busy day, I said.

Something t'eat? she asked.

Until I went to the bank I only had enough for a couple of coffees. I wanted one of those bit-stale yesterday buns Nora lets me have sometimes. But this morning she pulled a face.

They're for the mission man, Tooks, she said. He'll be here soon.

Just one, I insisted. They won't miss one.

Van doesn't like it. You know that.

He's not here, though, is he.

No, said Nora hesitatingly.

Well, what's the harm, then?

I felt better after the bun. Hunger gone. I ordered another coffee and sat for ages on my own in the increasingly warm morning sun outside Van Goff's, smoking a cigarette, watching the world — actually, the early-morning going-to-work people, dog-walkers, traffic and scooters of Ponsonby Road — go by, and thinking.

Turned out to be a day for thinking.

I admit I was thinking about 'It' because 'It' was, and had been for days, worrying me.

You okay, Tooks? asked Nora when she brought my second coffee.

Yeah, I said, looking up and nodding my thanks. I'm good.

She said I looked preoccupied or something.

Thinking, that's all, I said. Just thinking.

I was still thinking about 'It'. The last one.

Numbers One to Eleven were fine but Twelve? Something was bothering me about it and I didn't know what or why. It annoyed me intensely. I knew the feeling: intuition. I trusted it. Always had. But in this case I just couldn't figure it out. It doesn't matter now — all resolved thanks to that Lallemand bloke — but it mattered this morning. I felt I was running out of time.

She asked me if I was worried about tonight.

What, I wondered, did she know about tonight? Female intuition?

No way, love, I said. All done.

Well, take care, Tooks, eh. She sounded genuinely concerned. Why? And, hey— she pointed to my little trio of soft tobacco pack, papers and cowboy boot lighter — you smoke too much.

I laughed at that, which made me cough. Briefly. After which I said, pointing to my almost-empty packet of tobacco, Only baccy these day, love.

She must have known what I meant but she ignored that and asked me if I was going to get cleaned up for tonight.

That puzzled me again. Female intuition again? I didn't know.

What are you saying?

It's a big deal, Tooks, she said.

How do you know? I asked. Surprised. I didn't think anyone — Nora or Van or anyone — knew anything about tonight.

Ivan told me last night, she said. He guessed. The way you've been acting and that. That's what he said, anyway.

I didn't know what to say. Or think.

Trim your beard at least, she said as she stroked her own chubby chin. And your hair.

You my mother or something? I asked with a smile.

Nora laughed then. Mr Zelnick will be expecting it, you know, she said.

Another surprise. I asked her what she knew about Zenick.

Nothing, said Nora. It's just what Ivan said. He knows stuff, you know. He saw a poster or something.

That explained it: the posters.

Your old man knows nothing, I said with a laugh. And neither do you. And, anyway, I don't care what *Mister* Zelnick expects. Or what he thinks.

But then, even this morning, I secretly *did* care about Zelnick and what he thought. Because I then didn't know what to expect. It's easy now — now that it's all over — but Auckland's not London, Parnell's not the King's Road, and Zelnick's is not the notorious Chetwin-Lewis Gallery. So I was determined to look good for Zelnick. To not let him down. It was a bit of an experiment for me but I knew it was really important to him.

In all the world now, only *he* had me. And I had only him.

I finished my coffee and smoke and was about to get up — gathering together my little smoking troika — when Sherylene arrived and dropped heavily, clumsily, into the other chair at my table. Nearly half-past seven in the morning and he was wearing a black evening gown with fake pearls. And he needed a shave.

Spare a dollar or two, Tooks? he asked.

Come on, Sher, I said patiently. Do I look rich?

I didn't mind old Sherylene. Felt sorry for him, really. But that sort of cadging always annoys me, whoever's doing it.

A durrie then?

I pointed to my still tabled trio. Go on then, I said.

Sherylene looked at me questioningly, intently, and held up a V of two chubby fingers. The black but chipped nail polish depressed me.

I nodded.

Ta, Tooks, he said as he tremble-handedly rolled two generously fat cigarettes with his fat fingers, tremblingly lit one with my lighter and slipped the other into his Lurex evening bag.

You're all right, you know, he said after taking a long drag and pushing the tobacco packet — flat and limp — across the table.

I watched sadly as the strange and ageing he hobbled away, thick hairy calves, and fat feet forced into somewhat dirty shoes, dull and scuffed, with heels high enough to require a modicum of female poise and balance, neither of which the inelegant Sherylene had ever possessed. However, his ungainly hobbling departure — now familiar to me and my fellow Van Goff patrons — drew stares from those passers-by who were not locals.

Van here yet? I asked the girl inside — not Nora — taking the money.

No, said the girl, who avoided eye contact and seemed reluctant to engage in conversation. Did I look *that* old and awful to that young and pretty teen?

Nora?

Nah. Gone to get more milk. Low fat.

Oh, okay, I said, trying to be friendly and harmless but evidently not succeeding. I think I actually scared her. See ya.

See ya, said the girl, whose name doesn't matter.

My real name is Tookman. Tookman Julius Messenger. I was 'Julius' in London — just 'Julius' — but Tooks before and since.

I was named after my mother's father, Sir Tookman Julius Watney, whom I never met. He evidently made a fortune importing and selling farm machinery after the first world war and was later knighted by the National government for services to the rural economy (and the party), before he died in nineteen fifty-nine. According to my mother, who was just 18 when the old man died, he was adored, worshipped, by his daughters, each of whom named one of her children — not necessarily a son — Tookman. Thus, Tooks Messenger of Auckland, New Zealand — *moi* — late of London, England,

Europe generally, and America occasionally, has six unknown cousins, belonging to unknown aunts, with unknown surnames, scattered around the world, called Tookman Something. However, I've never met any of my same-name cousins despite having travelled all over the world, probably but unknowingly visiting their homelands.

Back on the street, I looked at my watch. Ten till eight. Looked up and down the street. All the shops were closed and dark except Van Goff's and Jana's fruit shop, farther up the road, but there were people everywhere. Cars and buses and trucks and couriers all going about their business, whatever it was. And more stiffly-upright young business people — male and female — all inappropriately dressed for whizzing along precariously, dangerously, on those tiny-wheeled electric scooters.

I couldn't help thinking of London.

Nine Thursday night in London. Now. Our lovely little flat in Hollywood Road, off the busy Fulham Road. My happy home with my happy Fiona. She would've just got in. I'd be all cleaned up but still smelling a bit of turps (as usual). I'd have dinner ready. How was her day? Fine, thanks, love. Usual. I'd show her my progress. She'd stand back and study it, whatever it was. Think. She had a good eye. What would Willoughby think? Say? We'd discuss that. And then, a fine spring night so we'd have the French doors open. Eat outside on the terrace.

I didn't really want to think about that sort of thing but as far as Fiona memories go they were better than the other sort, which still haunt me. Seeing her lying there under that cold hospital light. Three o'clock in the morning. Her face grey. Her lovely hair lank and lifeless. Such thoughts still come to me and make me shiver; it takes a conscious effort to dispel them. And then when I did, this morning — dispel thoughts of Fiona, what happened and what might have been — the vacant thought-space was immediately filled with 'It': Number Twelve.

A replacement thought that was both welcome and not.

I considered sitting quietly on the bench at the bus stop and having another smoke from my dwindling tobacco supply, but it was too busy there. People checking their phones, looking up and around occasionally, looking worried, angry, glancing up at the flickering bus schedule sign, jiggling their legs, turning over their HOP card, waiting impatiently for the next bus. Everyone, except me, with somewhere to go, something to do.

I crossed College Hill Road to the old post office, now a trendy restaurant, and there, down Saint Mary's Bay Road, found a sunny spot in the little park beside the historic 'Ponsonby Fire Brigade Station'. It's an old building — nineteen hundred-and-three — with few redeeming features but I'm glad it's still there. It's been a restaurant for as long as I can remember. After getting my smoking trio out of my jeans, I sat on a bench and rolled another thin and stringy cigarette. And there I sat in the sun, puffing slowly, absent-mindedly, on my smoke, checking the burning end occasionally for no reason, diddling it with the tip of my little finger, daring it to burn me, while trying to think of nothing.

4.

I ESPECIALLY DIDN'T want to think about London and Fiona, or Mr and Mrs Gallacher — you can call me Mother if you like, said Fiona's mother — or the closed gallery and Willoughby's mysterious disappearance, and me getting interviewed by the fraud squad while dealing with the funeral and Fi's parents. Then the flat and the pompous young estate agent, and the sale to some bloody Arab, and still waiting for the money. Rather, I tried to think positively about it all. Perhaps Willy had good news about the money: the flat all settled and Chetwin-Lewis found and jailed, and coughing up almost all he owed, and a grovelling apology from Coutts.

In the end, though, I couldn't help thinking only about Zelnick and, with mild anxiety, the end of the day, The Twelve and, inevitably, the unknown problem with Number Twelve.

I couldn't help it about Number Twelve.

I knew — at least hoped — it was something minor that would bother only me, something no one else would even notice. Something small, tiny, insignificant, like a grain of grit in your shoe. Tiny to the eye but irritatingly annoying only to the shoe-wearer, so irritating that it must be found and disposed of. But I couldn't dispose of it until I found it. I knew it was there — something unsettling, disturbing, spoiling what should have been a relaxing day — but I had no idea what it was.

Intuition is not knowledge. In the past, when I had intuition Fiona had knowledge. I knew that with certainty. But Fiona is—

No! I said to myself. I'm not bloody well going over that again. I'm here now. This is my home. I have to depend on myself. If there is something wrong — or at least something not quite right — with Number Twelve then I need to find it for myself. Meanwhile I should be having a quiet, relaxing, pleasant day before the drama of tonight.

Suddenly, my phone came to life. Vibrated in my pocket. A muffled Pink Floyd breaking into my somewhat unhappy reverie.

Sitting down, I couldn't get the phone out of the front pocket of my jeans. I flicked away the wet and stained butt of my tiny cigarette, stood up and awkwardly dug into my jeans pocket to retrieve the phone, which brightly told me it was Gregan. Seeing that, I wished I didn't have to answer it.

I don't care for Gregan. I never have. But for the last year or so I've had no choice: I've had to put up with him. I was obligated to him. It was my own fault. But, thankfully, after tonight, after Uncle Frank, I can be free of him. I'll be telling him tomorrow or Sunday.

The obligation came from a decision I made only the day after I arrived from London just after that miserable Christmas on my own. Exhausted from flying Economy, I stayed one night in a cheap Fort St backpackers before contacting Willy about the money and everything. He said that Gregan knew I was home. How he knew I'll never know. Well, you know Gregan, said Willy. Anyway, he said you can stay in one of his flats until you get settled. In Clarence Street. Apparently it's furnished, ready to go. You can have it cheap, he said. Not a bad offer while we wait for everything to get settled.

And so I did that. I stayed in one of Gregan's nasty little flats — this one — hoping it wouldn't be long. Turned the bedroom into a studio and slept in the little sitting room. But it's taken more than a year for Willy to sort out everything in England with Coutts, the courts and the estate agent.

Gregan and I were at school together. Kings. Boarding. Because we both came from old Waikato farming families, Gregan thought we should be friends. But Willy — Paul Wilbraham

— was my only friend at Kings and neither of us liked Gregan. He never got the message and was always hanging around us. Now, forty-five years later, he had somehow managed to make me feel both obligated to him and guilty.

I went to his place in Lincoln Street — a huge, two-storey, Victorian mansion squeezed onto a tiny piece of land — to pick up the key to the flat, and immediately regretted my flat-taking decision. I saw and sensed at once that the Gregan who opened the door was merely the sixty-year-old version of the fifteen-year-old boy I once despised. As an adult, though, meeting Gregan after so many years, having had a lifetime of experience with some of the world's most unpleasant, conceited, rich, famous, spoiled and ego-centric people — including that time in New York with Bernadine — I knew on that first day in Lincoln Street exactly what was (and is) wrong with Gregan: he is a dreadful narcissist.

As a boy, I didn't know why I disliked Gregan. My parents thought we should be friends, apparently having so much in common — which shows how well they knew me — and, of course, they were friends with the Gregan family in Matamata. But I couldn't help it. There was something about the boy Gregan that gave me the creeps. And I wasn't alone: Willy felt the same. Of course, I didn't know anything about narcissism then — didn't even know the word or its meaning — but I recognized the adult Gregan's condition as soon as I met him to pick up the key to the flat. But it was too late then.

Only now, after all this time, can I afford my own place and so free myself from my Gregan obligation.

I also learned, but later and not from him, that Gregan, who had once had a successful career as a sharebroker, had later inherited his family's farms. He was a spoiled only child, answerable to no one, and so he sold everything and has been living off the proceeds of his presumably clever and profitable investments ever since. He now lives alone but has been divorced by two wives: they and his four children — three by wife one and one by wife two — and two grandchildren, will have nothing to do with him. They had obviously learned, as I have, that a complete and uncompromising break is the only way to escape the cruelty and trauma of living and coping with a narcissist.

'No Contact' is the professional term.

I have often seen the cruel effects of narcissism on innocents and was myself cleverly manipulated once — by the beautiful, charming but ultimately evil and notorious Bernadine Galingale in New York — and so have learned to recognize and avoid narcissists. But on that day, the day I got the key to the flat, it was too late: I was broke, needed somewhere cheap to live, and so became heavily indebted to Gregan.

Narcissists love obligations like that. They also like to make their victims feel sorry for them and guilty for not helping them more over some alleged slight or suffering. In this case, Gregan told me — almost the first thing he said — that he had cancer. He said he was seeing a specialist — a private consultant, the best in the country, top in his field, he said — and was going to get treatment with a drug especially imported from Switzerland that was not generally available in New Zealand. He said he could get it from a special source he knew in Zurich. Costs a fortune but worth it.

All typical narcissist talk. And probably not even true.

Actually, I've tried to avoid him but I had to see him today. He sort of guilted me into it. When he told me again, as he always does, how ill he's been, it almost certainly annoyed him that I didn't ask for details or show any sympathy. I still don't know if he really has cancer — and if he does where or what it is — but after talking to him today, when he was pretty well drunk, I'm sure that if he is ill then at least cancer's not the cause.

Anyway, I answered the phone. Tried to sound cheerful. But I wasn't concentrating. I was admiring — I always had — the old Ley's Institute library and gymnasium buildings across the road. Originally gifted to the city in nineteen-hundred-and-five, by some wealthy and well-meaning citizen, they stand together as authentic examples of the Edwardian pride that tried but couldn't quite abandon the Victorian love of architectural decoration.

Gregan wanted to know where I was and what I was doing. Why, I don't know. Actually, I was only half-listening to the phone while I studied the old buildings. I told him I'd just had breakfast at Van Goff's and he wanted to know if I was going to call in to see him.

I've been really crook, he said. Feeling worse. In bed for two days. Wouldn't mind some company.

He sounded desperate, like he actually *needed* me for something. Foolishly, I half-believed him. Should have known better. Anyway, I told him I had a few things to do — I didn't know about the money then — but I could call in later if necessary.

Then he wanted to know what 'things' I had to do. Typical Gregan. Typical narcissist.

Just things, I said. I was actually annoyed by his tone and unwilling to share anything personal. So I told him I'd call in as soon as I could and he wanted to know — insisted — when that might be. I said about lunch time. Then he asked me to get him a pie and a cream doughnut for lunch.

Really? I asked. Haven't you been ill? Can you really eat that stuff?

Even as I asked, I wondered why I should even care about his diet when he obviously didn't.

He said he shouldn't but did anyway. Then he asked me about tonight. Was I okay.

I was surprised that Gregan even remembered or cared about what was happening outside his own narcissistic ego-centric cancer-obsessed world. Even more surprised that he cared to ask after my feelings until I remembered — so easy to forget — that narcissists always know what's the very 'right' thing to say and do while never actually caring at all.

I said everything was cool. Said I was going to have a haircut for the occasion. Then he wanted to know where I was going for a haircut. Wanted to recommend someone he knew in Surrey Crescent.

Your loss, mate, he said when I brushed off his Surrey Crescent hairdresser friend suggestion.

I could have said something about my Number Twelve doubts, as I might have said to a *real* friend, but I didn't. I knew that Gregan — like all narcissists — could and would remember and exploit, somehow at some time, any hint of doubt or anxiety which he would happily interpret as a weakness. I didn't want to give him the pleasure.

Anyway, he said, don't forget: pie — mince and cheese — and that doughnut.

5.

I CHECKED THE time before I rejeaned the phone. It was still only about ten past eight. Three Lamps was still busy. Seems it's always busy. But, then, not really: I had to remind myself of the busyness I *used* to know, took for granted, on the Fulham Road, King's Road and Sloan Square. Seemed like another world, another life.

I knew Willy couldn't see me for at least an hour so I slumped back to the bench to have another smoke and think.

Gregan's call had annoyed me. It was enough to be worried about Number Twelve, but now Gregan. Somehow, I was now obliged to buy lunch and share it with one of the least likeable people I know. Not for the first time I wished that Gregan really *did* have cancer and would die soon. That would save me from the unpleasantness of a complete break — an irrevocable release from a friendship I'd never wanted — which I knew I'd have to make one day.

I didn't know about Uncle Frank then. But I knew, this morning, and am certain now, that when I quit this flat I won't tell Gregan about my move to Dunedin. It's highly unlikely he'd follow me there, or look me up for any reason, but I need to make sure I never have anything to do with him again. Ever.

But what, I thought, what if he really does have cancer? I shook my head then, to shake off the thought. I know from personal experience what *real* cancer looks like. Before Fiona, I had seen it in many people — young and old, including friends — in London. And now, after seeing Gregan at lunchtime today, I'm sure he's faking it for sympathy and attention.

Why on earth would someone do that?

Meanwhile, poor old Uncle Frank, Father's only remaining sibling and my only living New Zealand relative, really did have cancer. Old, sad, sick and mildly demented, he had always been especially kind to me. Looked after me when I came to Auckland all those years ago. I stayed with him and Auntie Joyce. They even let me set up a studio in my bedroom, where I continued to paint my way through my half-hearted architectural studies.

Father despised his brother Frank much as he despised me, and for much the same reason. Thinking about it all this morning — cancer and Uncle Frank — made me resent the faking Gregan even more.

I called in to see Bill Jana, who was unpacking bananas and arranging them on display under the neon lights and angled mirrors of his shop. Like Willy and Gregan, I knew Bill from school. He was a clever kid then, especially with maths, and everyone thought he'd grow up to be a scientist or a mathematician, or something else clever, but he ended up inheriting his father's Three Lamps fruit shop.

He looked up without stopping his banana-stacking work when he realized I wasn't a customer.

I asked him how he was, how things were going, and he told me that the supermarket's giving him and Anton the shits. I didn't know who Anton was — is — so he told me he owned the dairy up the road. Anton's Dairy.

Bill worked hard, really hard, I could see that. I thought, God, he's been doing this since he left school. While I've been swanning around London, around the world, making money, losing money, getting ripped off, getting somewhat famous, in rehab, getting married and widowed, he's been working his arse off here in this drab little Ponsonby fruit shop.

He worked as we talked but I could sense he was preoccupied, not really interested in me. Eventually, he stopped to fling an empty banana box into the corner of the shop, where others lay in an angular jumble of brown cardboard. I couldn't help admiring the banana-grower's blue and yellow logo which had been so carefully designed but so carelessly printed on the coarse cardboard.

He paused then, lifted his green apron to wearily wipe his hands, and said that it couldn't last. He and the dairy would soon be out of business. And then what? he asked. That's what I'd bloody-well like to know.

He sounded angry and I suddenly felt in the way. But then, quickly, he relaxed, apologized, and asked me how I was. What I'd been up to. He sounded genuine. I suppose he was. I told him I'd been as busy as a bastard. Finished now, though, I said.

But you've been away, he said. Haven't seen you for a while.

It was as if, to him, the last twenty years might have been twenty days. I told him I'd been in London. Painting as usual, he said, rather than asked. I thought I might tell him about things: about Chetwin-Lewis and Fiona and coming home and The Twelve. He sounded interested at first but I soon realized he was merely being polite, nodding mechanically. His thoughts were obviously elsewhere. Had his own worries.

Obviously, having suddenly turned up after twenty years, looking all hairy and unkempt, sounding more English than Kiwi, without explanation, I was probably a mystery he didn't care to solve while being preoccupied with his own business worries.

And, anyway, there was a lady customer waiting. And when he said, Mate, I better get cracking, I realized that he didn't even remember my name.

Back on the street I felt rejected, vaguely dejected, selfish and guilty. I should have asked busy, worried Bill about his own life. No doubt he got married and had kids, grandies even, a house and a mortgage, but now I'll probably never know. There was I, with nothing to do all day, while he was busy, and not a little worried about his business. Like everyone in the world, he was carrying his own heavy bag of troubles. Why should he care about me and mine?

I checked my watch again: quarter past eight.

After, what, more than a year of hard and constant work I found it hard to believe I still had a full day ahead with almost nothing to do. It looked empty. A meeting with Willy (for what? I was hopeful but unsure); lunch (meaning a pie and doughnut with Gregan); Davy for the haircut; Uncle Frank, of course, (no doubt having to deal with his banjo and 'Old Man'); and that's it. Then back to the flat for something to eat before Zelnick and everything that would go with it and after it.

Zelnick was optimistic. I knew that. I also knew that he knew what he was talking about; if he was optimistic then I should be, too. But I still had that lingering, annoying, intuitive doubt about Number Twelve.

Before I left New Zealand, during those nearly twenty years as a 'struggling young artist', I knew *of* Zelnick, had even visited his gallery — in a Newmarket back street then — but I'd never actually met him and thought, back then at least, that I'd never be good enough for his gallery. While I was away, though, his gallery had grown enormously and his reputation had reached me in London just as mine had reached him in Auckland. When I got back and approached him, I found he had a fine gallery in a great Parnell location and a priceless customer list.

Nevertheless, foolishly, I still had my doubts. Auckland's not London, I thought. Parnell's not King's Road, and Mort Zelnick is not Willoughby Chetwin-Lewis (which is probably just as well).

It's all over now. Tonight was fine for us both. I can say that now, sitting quietly, at the end of the day, writing and smoking, my tea gone cold, with only the now-sleeping Jaws for company. Obviously, I should have had more confidence in myself, as well as in Zelnick, but after Fiona and the whole Chetwin-Lewis bullshit, I *lacked* confidence. I can see that now. I was needlessly worried — this morning and all day — having no idea it would work out so well.

All I knew for certain was that I was uncertain, especially about Number Twelve.

I found myself at All Saints. I sat on one of the low scoria rocks that in a line mark the boundary of the church's land. I sat facing the front, my back to the street.

I love fine buildings and fine architecture but All Saints church, Ponsonby, is not a fine building. It was built in nineteen fifty-seven, probably to replace something wooden and traditional that almost certainly looked like a real church. It has a grand entrance, which I can't help admiring, that's reminiscent of the front of a Māori whare but whether that was accidental or intentional I don't know.

I know a bit — quite a lot — about buildings, construction and architecture, ancient and modern, thanks to Father's insistence (although I didn't thank him at the time).

Across and up the road I could see the high, slender and green-patinaed steeple of Saint John's. It's unmistakably a church — a 'proper' church, if you like — built in good old New Zealand kauri and dedicated to one saint, not 'all' saints. And Scots presbyterian, not English Anglican.

But I see it's now for sale. I wonder who'll buy it and what they'll do with it. It's a large building, so it must have once been supported by a large congregation. But few people go to these traditional churches any more. I know the Polynesian churches are always full, as are the weird, sect-like evangelical churches, which seem more political than spiritual, and designed to exploit for money the doubts and fears of their naïve and innocent followers, but I wonder if anyone is really serious about conventional and traditional Christianity any more.

Whatever their denomination, old and traditional New Zealand churches look architecturally attractive but are in fact a bit weird. The early Auckland settlers, inevitably devout Christians, came to the colonies and built their churches in the only style they knew. But in the absence of stone they used wood — of which there was plenty — fashioned to imitate stone. *Faux* Saxon? *Faux* Norman? *Faux* Gothic?

Real churches in England, from the Anglo-Saxon middle ages through the Norman conquest right up to Victorian times — England is full of them (mostly empty) — were so beautifully designed to start with, always true to a design tradition, and built of stone to last millennia. They'll still be there when Saint John's Over The Road is no more than a pile of rotten wood, although I must admit that the copper roof of the steeple will still be there if it doesn't get stolen. At least your All Saints in front of me is made of concrete and bricks, which increases its chances of survival.

Suddenly I couldn't believe how my thoughts were wafting around so dreamily: the architecture of churches, ancient and modern, in England and New Zealand. I was *so* bored. I felt as though I could easily fall asleep, sitting there in the morning sun, if it weren't for the sharp hardness of the rock digging into my thin and bony arse.

I stood up then to escape the bottom pain, and wondered what I should do next.

6.

AS I'VE SAID before, I've always been busy: an adult lifetime of busyness. And then, even with Fiona gone, or rather because she was gone, there was so much more to do. I was so busy I had no time to think. A good thing? I thought so then but now I'm not sure. Maybe I should have slowed down a bit, should have allowed more time to properly grieve. That's what Mrs Barkstone says, anyway.

People wanted to help me. They meant to be kind but I shoved them away. There was so much to do on my own. So hard without Fiona. Dealing with the whole complicated money thing between Coutts, Chetwin-Lewis and the police — even Interpol at one point — all involving Willy at a great distance, although he did come to London once. Then selling the flat and working with the estate agent. Sorting out everything with Fiona's parents wasn't easy, either. They were well over eighty and had never been out of Scotland, which meant they were utterly overwhelmed by London while having to grieve for their daughter — their only

44

child — and deal with all the dreadful circumstances of her death, not to mention the financial complexities and consequences of her marriage to the strange New Zealand artist — they hardly knew me, really — his complicated financial problems and his determination to have everything sorted out before he left England permanently.

But we so wanted to get to know you, lad, said the old, pipe-puffing Mr Gallacher in the empty, echoing flat where we stood awkwardly together after the funeral. You were such an important part of wee Fi's life, you know. There's so much you could tell us about the last few years. Her poor mother wants to ask you so much. But now—

I had apologised as best I could. I liked Fiona's parents. We holidayed with them in Dundee sometimes, especially during those Edinburgh Festival years. Fiona said they were somewhat overawed to see me being interviewed on television.

I didn't like to hurt them, as I understood what they wanted from me, sympathized with them. I tried to explain that I had no reason to stay in England any more. I've done everything I set out to do, I said, although I didn't bother them with the Chetwin-Lewis business: Fiona had kept it from them so I followed her example. And now, without Fiona, I said, there's no point any more. Well, you will stay in touch, won't you, said a teary Mrs Gallacher as

I bent to kiss her fondly on her old and over-powdered cheek.

And then, since arriving from London — after so long, too long, away — I hadn't stopped. Gregan's flat. Living on what Willy Wilbraham managed to get me from the trust. Setting up a studio from scratch. More than a year working on The Twelve while keeping out of sight.

It was widely accepted in London that I'd left England. Had a breakdown after the closure of the gallery. Chetwin-Lewis's disappearance, they said. Money problems. And then his wife. So he dropped out, they said. But where the hell he went they seemed to neither know nor care.

From what I can tell, reading the English papers on my phone, the red-tops are still vitally interested in the disgraced Chetwin-Lewis — they really *love* a posh scandal — but Fiona and I are never mentioned, apparently all but forgotten. So nobody in England — or Europe or America — now knows or cares where Julius is, or what he's doing, which suits me fine. And those few people here who think they know me actually don't know much. Why should they? They just know I was away for a few years — how many they don't know, and doing exactly what they couldn't guess and anyway don't care — and was back sounding a bit English and looking a lot like an old 'sixties hippy. Tall, thin and wiry, hairy, heavily wrinkled, always smoking. An artist, or something.

Suits me.

I needed another smoke. Where to go? I looked around and then set off aimlessly.

I remembered Costley Park. I hadn't thought of it for years. I decided to walk down there, have a smoke. The only problem: I knew it'd be an easy downhill walk but a hard uphill walk back. I thought — knew — I'd get puffed out but decided it would be worth it. A peaceful sit, a quiet smoke, nice surroundings, time to think.

Or not think.

I've understated it so far but the money really *was* a big deal — worth thinking about — although I didn't know anything for sure until Willy opened his office at nine, and it wasn't even half past eight. Call in a bit after nine, he'd said. Quarter past. Always a few things to do Friday mornings but I'll be free by quarter past. Plus, we can have a yarn. A catch up. A debriefing. After all—

It didn't take long to walk down Russell Street. I stopped at the top of the park and sat on a bench overlooking the little playground, which looked empty and sad without children. After all, children are the very reason for a playground. Without them the whole place seemed pointless and utterly silent without their excited squealing and laughing. The idle swings hung heavy, steady and still, while the single see-saw stood stoically, patiently, one T-handled end in the air as if trying to attract attention. And they all — the slides and roundabouts, too — looked merely chipped and rusty, their once-gaudy colours faded, oxidized and dull, and randomly decorated with sticky, damp leaves, yellow and brown. It reminded me of the rides and amusements standing idle and half-covered with ancient tarps at English seaside resorts during the winter. Without people, they looked merely tawdry, sad and depressing, a sight that failed to lift my mood.

I rolled, lit and drew on another thin cigarette, blew blue smoke into the cool, still, damp and bush-scented air, looked out over the playground to the path that wound down to Georgina Street through the old and lanky mānuka trees, and tried to empty my mind.

Despite what some people say and advise, I've always found it impossible to think of nothing. And so, with nothing to do but sit and smoke, I involuntarily resumed thinking. Indeed, today's been a day for thinking.

I realized lately — actually it came to me as I was finishing Number Twelve — that all my life, while I was working, and even while I was planning to work, thinking about a new painting, or a series, my thinking was of a distinct character. I could even describe the place in my head (or brain or mind) where it was done: towards the back, a bit to the right. Now, with nothing to do but think, I felt that my lazy and unfocussed thinking of the type I was doing then and all morning — nothing to do with planning or painting or anything even faintly intellectual — was occurring in no particular part of the mind but rather bouncing and bumping around against the inside of my skull, free and uncontrolled, randomly picking up loose thoughts before discarding them and rushing on. It was — and is — an unfamiliar and undisciplined way of thinking. But it wasn't unpleasant and so, with nothing else to do, nothing else to think about, I let my mind wander as it might.

Apart from the matter of the money, which I hoped would be resolved soon, and the lingering doubt about Number Twelve, which would *not* be dismissed, my main thought then was of the end of day, the evening, and how far away — in time — it then seemed. And yet, for more than a year now, since I'd been back, no day had seemed long enough; I'd always been busy.

In London — and New York and Paris, too — there might have been time to think, if I'd made it, but I'd had no need. Chetwin-Lewis was always there from the beginning, directing me, managing me, telling me what to do, where to go, what to say, and to whom. Meanwhile Fiona did all the 'us' thinking. All I had to do was paint and show up at the gallery and at parties and functions and interviews when and where Willoughby and Fiona said.

That, I knew, was the root of my today problem. All those years when I didn't have to think about anything. Fame — modest fame but fame all the same — interviews and invitations, merchandising and royalties, and sales, of course, all came easily and quickly. Some would say too easily and quickly. And, with it all, bucket-loads of money. So welcome after years of struggle at home.

At that time I had nothing but contempt for the homeland which had pretty much ignored me. London was definitely the place for me. Then. But now. This, I thought — meaning Ponsonby (not Chelsea), Parnell (not the King's Road), Zelnick (not W C-L), dollars (not pounds) — is altogether better. Except. Except Fiona. I still miss her. Every day. Actually I could weep with missing her even now, sitting alone in the gloom with nothing but the sleeping Jaws for company.

Nothing or nobody will ever replace her.

Strangely, I am a better person for what I went through, and a better person here than I ever was in London, where I was in danger of becoming a rich and arrogant prick. Fiona saw it coming and didn't like it. She tried to tell me, help me, but then she got sick.

I *know* she would approve of the new me. If only she were here to see it.

Suddenly I realized that my random thinking had once again settled on memories of Fiona; wonderful times past but recent memories that are not pleasant. Thoughts and visions of her sad ending had squeezed out all thoughts of Number Twelve.

I decided I'd rather be worried about Number Twelve — rather be worried about anything — than be thinking about Fiona. So I made myself think about it — Number Twelve — again, and the idea that I had no idea what was wrong with it. What was worrying my subconscious was somehow comforting when compared with the Fiona thoughts. Meanwhile there was nothing I could do. Nothing could happen until tonight. And that was still hours away.

I stood up then, flicked away the burning ciggie butt, and walked across to the set of swings — the once-yellow-painted wooden seats worn smooth by thousands of small bottoms — and launched one emptily into the air. Number Twelve fought with Fiona for my attention as I watched the empty swing swinging and wobbling, its arc quickly decaying without a passenger to both steady it and urge it on.

Thankfully, Number Twelve won. But I still had no idea what was wrong. On the contrary: to me, even then, it was perfect; the culmination of all that came before. Not just One to Eleven but everything, including everything I did in London, Paris and New York, now hanging in galleries and private mansions all over Europe and America. It — Number Twelve — was the last of the latest. And yet something was wrong.

7.

ALL THAT THINKING — about the past, present and future — led me to think again about money. It's only thanks to Willy that since I got back I've not gone completely short.

Father always complained that we were asset rich/cash poor but as a child I never thought we were *ever* short of money. Kings must have cost a lot. To be honest, looking back I suppose we were downright rich.

Father supported me generously after I was expelled from school for smoking. I went home then and worked on the Long Farm, helping with the milking twice a day, and otherwise worked as a general dogsbody for Cyril, the Home Farm manager.

By then, I had decided to be an artist, a painter. I had a small studio at home and specialized, even then, in painting buildings, especially abandoned and derelict farm cottages and out-buildings as well as old country pubs, farm supply stores, stock yards, and the area's monumental and appallingly ugly dairy factories and wool scouring works. But Father refused to sanction such a course and instead enrolled me in the nearest thing to 'art' that he — a tough, non-nonsense dairy farmer — could think of as a true career. Thus, after a couple of wasted years, dependent on Father, forced to do routine farm work, I found myself living with Uncle Frank and Auntie Joyce while studying architecture at the university of Auckland. I was an architectural student for only a year but what I learned was a fine ground upon which to paint my way from obscurity to eventual recognition and success.

Father never fully forgave me for leaving the farm but it wasn't until Mother died that he altogether gave up trying to control me. Mother never recovered from losing little Rosamund, who was only ten, in nineteen seventy-two, when she died of meningitis. Then, when Mother herself died ten years later — of a broken heart everyone said — Father, weak and distraught, finally relented and let me transfer to art school. That was in nineteen eighty-three when I was nineteen and still living with Uncle Frank and Auntie Joyce.

Then I met Romola at art school.

I left Uncle Frank's then and moved into Romola's squalid little flat in Grey Lynn. Commercial Road. She was waitressing at a vegetarian restaurant in K Road while I got a part-time job at the John Leech gallery — thanks to my water-colour tutor, who was somehow related to the owner — where I learned something about fine art, a lot about picture framing, and even more about the people on whom all galleries and artists depend.

Romola and I both tried to paint in the flat between exploring, with others, the murky university-based world of music, alcohol and drugs. But while I paddled in the shallows of that dangerous sea, Romola chose to dive in head first and was soon lost to the art world. She left me, the flat, her job, university and Auckland, halfway through our second year and ended up working as an art director for some dodgy advertising agency in Wellington. I never saw her again. I wonder now whatever happened to her.

Willy and I were still friends then, although I don't know how he put up with me, especially when he was earnestly studying while I was with Romola and her spaced-out friends. But he did, which was just as well. It was about then, in my second year at art school, that Willy joined his father in the family law firm.

When I first went to university I got a generous allowance, which Father continued, reluctantly, even when I transferred to art school. But it all stopped when I dropped out. Father was furious. As a result I spent the next twenty years in poverty and obscurity in Auckland, sharing flats, taking odd jobs, trying to find time to paint, seeking recognition which never came.

Then, having managed at last to get to London, I suddenly found wealth and fame thanks to Willoughby, who had inherited the Chetwin-Lewis gallery and was looking for new talent. That was my life for twenty easy and exciting years.

It was there, at Chetwin-Lewis, that I met Fiona. We didn't get on at first. But I did get on well with Julie. Julie Ambermere. We met where she worked, at a wine bar in Chelsea. We even lived together for a while. She was younger than me — thirty-five — and wanted children, which definitely didn't appeal to me. She left me for a cellist in the London Philharmonic.

Then there was that dreadful few months in New York — Chetwin-Lewis had a gallery there — where I somehow got involved with the narcissistic Bernadine Galingale, an off-off-Broadway actress. She was only 28 and hugely sexual. A nymphomaniac, I suppose. She taught me a lot about sex but even more about the perils of living with a real narcissist. Narcissistic personality disorder is truly the enemy of human relationships. Bernadine also drank too much, which meant that for those months with her I, too, drank too much until—

Well, with the help of a therapist and AA, I gave up drinking after that and haven't had a drop of the stuff since.

When Father died in 2012 I came back for his funeral. It was then I reconnected with Uncle Frank and realized that he was my only living relative in New Zealand. That was the only time I ever came home. Fiona stayed in London. We agreed that she should, that a rushed funeral trip wasn't the best way to see New Zealand, and that one day we'd do it properly. In the end she never saw the country that shaped her husband.

My darling Fiona.

She was a year older than me, and a lot wiser (which wasn't hard). She was Willoughby's version of Mrs Barkstone. Although she didn't care for me at first, she did make it her professional business to protect me from Willoughby's worst impulses, advise me personally, look after my finances and other interests in general, until, inevitably, well, we fell in old-fashioned love and got married. God, we were so in love. I've never experienced anything like it. Never will again.

We should have lived happily ever after.

Now I'd give all the money I've ever had, all the money I'll soon have, and all the money I'll ever have, if only—

It was only after Fiona died, when I was planning to come home, that I learned about Chetwin-Lewis's abrupt disappearance, which had left the business broke and my bank account empty. How he did that I'll never know but I *do* know it never would have happened if Fiona hadn't been ill.

As if I wasn't stressed enough — dealing with her absence — I suddenly found that I needed money for the first time in my London life. I was utterly broke — it was like being a student again — at least until I could sell the flat. In need of money, I discovered from Willy — we were in constant touch — that before he died Father had sold everything and created a trust of which Uncle Frank was now the sole beneficiary.

Willy only knew about it because my father had engaged *his* father to set up and administer the trust, a role which had then been inherited by Willy. Evidently, my father had always admired Willy's father who, until late nineteen eighty-one, was the 'Son' in Wilbraham and Son. He only knew him through my school friendship with Willy — whom he always rightly called Paul — but he admired the older man, Harry, Willy's father, and so became a long-term client, never guessing that Harry's son would one day inherit power over his precious trust.

Willy also told me, for the first time, that Uncle Frank was in an expensive care home in Ponsonby being paid for by the trust of which he, Willy — or at least Wilbraham and Son — was the administrator, and from which I was excluded until Uncle Frank was dead when, but not before, I would become the sole beneficiary.

Willy didn't think that was right, and neither did I, for that matter.

It turned out that unlike his father — Wilbraham senior — Willy's not much of a criminal lawyer. But he's fantastic at everything else. So it was he who slowly and meticulously unpicked his father's somewhat sloppy work, in the courts, to loosen the trust's grip on the Messenger fortune.

I didn't (and don't) begrudge poor old Uncle Frank his dementia care but until everything got sorted in London I really needed some money. And so, while Fiona was ill and suffering her futile treatment, and Willoughby was hiding away somewhere in Europe, Willy was busy working, at a great distance, with Coutts, their London lawyers, and the police, who were chasing Chetwin-Lewis all over the continent. He also spent many hours in the New Zealand courts on my behalf, getting things 'put right' as the judge apparently said. As a result I received — and still receive — a small monthly allowance from the trust which has been enough to pay my rent (to Gregan), to start up a studio from scratch, to buy sufficient food for me and Jaws, and a new wardrobe of old clothes to suit the new me. Willy also lent me the deposit to secure the Saint Clair cottage.

Now, of course, now that everything in England has been finalized, it doesn't matter about the trust. Nevertheless, according to what Willy told me, I'm now fully entitled to the annuity which had been Uncle Frank's. Then, when I go, the trust's capital will be divided between the Salvation Army and the Meningitis Foundation, both my mother's favourites.

Meanwhile, thanks to Willy again, I've got almost everything back from England — from the bank and the sale of the flat — plus, after tonight, Zelnick will owe me more than a bank manager's annual salary.

Looks like I'll never be broke again. Rather, I can now quit Gregan's nasty little flat, buy a car, pay Willy back and move to my little Saint Clair cottage.

However, this morning, before I knew what I now know, I knew I had only enough in the bank to get a much-needed fresh packet of tobacco, something nice for Uncle Frank, a haircut from Davy, pies and doughnuts to share with Gregan and, later, a taxi to Zelnick's and another one home.

I checked my watch then and it was still only a quarter till nine. I thought about another cigarette but apart from being almost out of tobacco I knew it was an uphill walk back to Ponsonby Road. I decided to wait for a smoke also thinking, admitting I suppose (reluctantly) that Nora was probably right.

You smoke too much, she said.

I shook my head then, literally, in an attempt to shake off the unwelcome thought which lately comes to me often, the result an unbusy mind. The thing is, I can't imagine life without smoking; couldn't face it, in fact. It was enough to have given up all the other stuff, everything that was everywhere in London, including booze. In the end, though, giving it all up was surprisingly easy seeing how it helped Fiona — she'd already been through it — and I've got no regrets. Willoughby was worried for a while but contrary to expectations, including my own, my work actually improved. Everyone said so, including the all-important 'market'.

But to never smoke tobacco again?

Mister Cancer is always tapping on my thoughts' door — as he does to every smoker — but, despite all the evidence, I almost always succeed in refusing him entry. Anyway, I always think — as I do now, late at night, having my last smoke of the day — look at Uncle Frank. Smoked all his life until the cancer (but not lung cancer), and the dementia which ironically caused him to forget the habit altogether. Eighty-nine and still playing and singing heartily — until tonight — much to the annoyance of his fellow residents.

I thought, as I exited the playground, about walking along Wood Street and then up Pember-Reeves to Ponsonby Road. And then immediately thought how ridiculous it was to even have the time to debate the subject of the easiest route for my return walk. Instead, I set off slowly for the top of Russell Street, where I planned to fill in time until Willy's office opened for business and me.

It's a steep walk up Russell Street, so by the time I reached the top it was after nine and I was breathing heavily — I knew that would happen — so I had to rest. I sat down on a low wall outside what used to be, but is no longer, a dentist's place, where I (don't laugh) rolled a cigarette.

I went to that dentist once. A long time ago. I had to. But I hated dentists and dentistry then and I still do. I suppose I'm not alone there.

I remember the last time I went to a dentist in London.

How much?! asked an astonished Fiona. She couldn't believe it and neither could I.

It was a Harley Street clinic recommended by Willoughby. Well, I never even met his professional friend. All I got was a painful scraping and poking and flossing by a young nurse employee and a lecture on the health risks of smoking and how it stains the teeth and ruins the gums.

Your gums are in pretty good condition for a smoker of your age, she said with an Essex accent and a toothy white, smuggy smile. But, to be honest, that's a matter of luck. If you're not careful, you'll have incurable gum problems and then dentures and we don't want that, do we?

Teeth and gums, I thought, as I fumbled in my jeans pocket for my smoking triumvirate. Another example of the lies we were told and are still being told.

I have many examples.

All through childhood we were told it's so important to brush your teeth. All those toothpaste brands telling us how important it was to brush our teeth to make them clean and WHITE. Having a white smile was essential. But then, later — and too late for many people — we learned that having white teeth isn't as important as flossing, and brushing away the tartar that migrates under the gums to cause inflammation, disease and bad breath, brushing not the teeth but the gums to stimulate them, to increase the blood circulation and so stop them shrinking and so exposing the soft parts of the teeth — unprotected by enamel — which decay away so easily. Next stop: dentures.

Well, we don't want that, do we.

Anyway, hate is too strong a word but I really don't like dentists and that's that. So I rolled another thin cigarette from the few remaining strands of tobacco hiding deep in the plastic packet, lit it and smoked it in a sort of childish defiance of all dentists, from Harley Street, London, W1G 6AQ, to Russell Street, Auckland,

0624. After all the addictions I've overcome — with Fi's support, yes, but in the end on my own, really — I'm not going to stop smoking, my last vice. And, thank goodness, I'll soon have new packet fat with fresh and fragrant tobacco.

Meanwhile, dentists and doctors can all get stuffed.

8.

AFTER MY SMOKE it was only a short stroll up to Ponsonby Terrace and down the fifty metres or so to Willy's office. It's not a real office but a drastically altered kauri Californian bungalow abomination. Actually that's not fair. I've got nothing against the underlying and iconic architectural style of the classic Californian bungalow. I admire its handsome look. I'm sure that the Wilbrahams' office would once have had a charm of its own derived from the proven and standard Californian bungalow design which, in lieu of a real architect, was no doubt faithfully copied by an unknown Auckland builder from a book of plans bought mail-order from a supplier in San Francisco, the design source of much of Auckland and New Zealand's suburban houses of that time, the late 'twenties/early 'thirties. Unlike the newly fashionable but utterly inappropriate Mediterranean look, the old Californian bungalow is perfectly designed — with steep roofs, wide overhanging eaves, and spacious covered verandas — for Auckland's hot and furniture-fading sun and drenching downpours of rain.

But the house-cum-office of Wilbraham and Son has no such appeal. It's been added to and taken away from so many times that what remains is utterly charmless. And where once there was a lawn, bounded no doubt by a picket fence and a border of pretty perennials, or perhaps a low hedge neatly trimmed with care by a proud owner, as lovingly proud of his new house as he was of his family, the Wilbrahams — the late Wilbraham senior or his even later father — had once laid cheap unreinforced concrete to serve as a client car park, which over the years has cracked under the weight of the parked cars, cracks which nature has naturally, inevitably, filled with vigorous and various weeds.

The house's once wide wooden stairs were long ago replaced by a poorly made brick and concrete affair which raised me to a small but elegantly proportioned veranda and the unlocked front door.

Inside, the wide entrance lobby serves as a reception. It's wood panelled and elaborately ceilinged but tastelessly over-painted a neutral cream. A wooden archway, opening to a long, wide and dark hallway, is flanked by luxuriant ladder ferns in antique-looking copper pots set on tall, black-lacquered jardinières.

The hall beyond leads to a series of mysterious rooms into which I have never been. Indeed, I've only ever been into the room off the right side of the lobby — once, like the matching room to the left, a spacious bedroom with bay windows looking onto the concreted front yard — which now serves as Willy's office. The other matching bedroom/office was once the domain of the founding Wilbraham, and later of his son, Willy's father, both now, like my own father, dead and buried. Willy — the father of two adult daughters who have no interest in law or the family firm — is now the only Wilbraham, although a mysterious partner specializing in criminal law, whom I have never met, occupies the other room.

This morning, the hall was guarded by a desked young woman, thin and wan, with a long face, long teeth with steel braces, long and thin legs, arms, fingers and nails, and long hair, straight and colourless; someone new whom I'd never met.

Is Willy in yet? I asked.

She, the new young receptionist, drew back her head and looked both puzzled and mildly disgusted.

Who? she asked.

She didn't know Willy's schoolboy epithet.

Mr Wilbraham, I said slowly. Mr Paul Wilbraham of Wilbraham and Son, barristers and solicitors etcetera, etcetera, blah-diddy-blah.

I probably sounded pretty rude and sarcastic. Stupid, really, but it just came out.

Oh, said the girl-child. Mr Wilbraham's with a client at the minute. He's not to be disturbed.

Well, don't you worry about that, love, I said, leaning forward, pushing back my hair before resting my knuckles on her desk in front of her keyboard. I pointed to the door to my right behind which I knew my friend was no doubt expensively advising a poor — soon to be poorer — worried client. Just pop in quickly, or phone him — I pointed to the phone on her desk — and tell him Tooks is here. That's me, I added with a wink. Tooks Messenger. He's expecting me. Knows what it's about.

But he said—

He won't mind, love, I said. Really. I'll wait here.

I dropped onto one of the two leather couches against the wall beside the coffee table upon which sat a low pile of magazines and a vase of fresh seasonal flowers of some sort. I wanted a smoke but knew I shouldn't, couldn't. And, anyway, I was nearly out of tobacco.

But I just *can't*, said the young, pretty and nervous receptionist from her desk. She was evidently but unduly intimidated by Willy, her boss. If she only knew — as I did — the lewd thoughts her very presence probably conjured in the mind of her employer who, aged sixty, is possibly about the same age as her grandfather. If she did, she would be more disgusted than intimidated. But then, I realized later, she was probably more intimidated by this other strange sixty-year-old — me, tall and thin, wild-haired and bearded, dressed in jeans and T-shirt — who was couch-slouching while holding but not looking at a *National Geographic*.

Suddenly, though, she pushed back her wheeled chair and hurried away down the gloomy hall behind her desk.

I thought that was a bit strange.

A few minutes later, Lynley, a remarkably plain middle-aged woman who's Willy's highly-reliable 'right-hand man', came striding down the hall looking somewhat annoyed.

I stood up quickly.

Lynley, I said.

Mister Messenger. She sounded stern. I have to tell you that you frightened the life out of poor Emily.

Who?

Emily Stone, our new receptionist. Making demands like that.

Like what? I only asked—

Never mind that now. She certainly sounded annoyed. I know what happened, she added.

But—

Look, I can't interrupt Paul now and that's that.

But he *told* me to come. Texted me, I protested, tapping my watch face. Just after nine he said.

He knew you were coming but he's unexpectedly tied up, said Lynley patiently. He can't help it, but he told me to tell you, look— she smiled unexpectedly and handed me a sealed manilla envelope, large and thick, which she had been holding behind her back —it's all done. All over. All in there.

I took the fat envelope.

Are you sure? I asked doubtfully. Really? I could hardly believe it.

Really, said Lynley, still smiling as she clasped her now free hands over her chest, took and expelled a deep breath, and nodded. It looked as though she was not only sharing my relief but was also subtly suggesting that she was the real author of this moment — she probably was — the one who had done the complex but essential international legal, clerical and accounting work necessary to bring about this successful conclusion, the one to be thanked.

Oh, she added suddenly, seriously, remembering, there's things to be signed etcetera, papers, formalities, but everything's in Paul's office. I'll sort it all out with Paul later.

Thank you, I said coolly, with a slight bow.

In fact, she could have no idea how truly grateful I was. But I returned the unopened envelope to the somewhat pleased and satisfied woman who took it with a puzzled look.

If you say it's definitely all done—

Oh, yes, Mr Messenger, she insisted. Interrupted. It's definitely all done. The money will be in your account by the end of day if it's not there already.

—then that's enough for me, I said. In fact, Lynley, I added, I definitely don't need the paperwork. Not now, anyway.

Oh, said a surprised and somewhat disappointed Lynley.

I really couldn't be bothered carrying that envelope around with me all day. I probably would have lost it.

Leave it with Willy and I'll get it later, I said. When I do all the paperwork stuff.

If you say so, she said. But, please, *please*, don't come in like that again. Bothering our staff. They don't know you as Paul and I do.

You don't know me at all, I thought, but said: I won't. I promise. So say sorry to—

Emily.

—yes. Say sorry to Emily from me. And thank *you*, Lynley May Manderson. For all your sterling work. Job well done.

The dear lady beamed and blushed with pride.

9.

SITTING ON THE cold, hard brick-and-concrete steps which led up to and down from the chambers of Wilbraham and Son, trying to roll a ciggy from the remains of my tobacco, I found that I was actually shaking, shivering uncontrollably. I could easily have cried — sobbed — there and then. Unbelievable.

I didn't, but I gave up trying to roll a cigarette as I felt as sickly and anxious as I felt on the days and weeks following Fiona. But I knew it wasn't dread, panic and grief that was gripping me this morning but *relief*, huge relief. An emotional reaction I hadn't expected.

But then, this morning, after all that's happened, I knew it was over at last. I knew the sad and sordid details would be set out, line by line, in meticulous legal and accounting detail, in the documents and statements contained in the heavy manilla envelope lying on a desk or in a file somewhere in the office behind me. But I didn't need to see them. I needed only to know that it was all over. That settlement had been received on the flat; that Fiona's parents had been satisfied; that the case had been won against Chetwin-Lewis (whose principal was now no doubt being housed somewhere unpleasant at His Majesty's pleasure) and its bankers; that, at last, I had no more ties or obligations in the UK and that, thanks to the Metropolitan Police, Interpol, and especially Wilbraham and Son and their London and Edinburgh associates, everything had been settled and a small fortune — now in New Zealand dollars — was waiting in my new New Zealand bank account.

I don't what I would have done without Willy.

I can't remember who at school gave Willy his nickname. I'm not sure I ever knew. Things like that just seem to happen mysteriously at boys' schools. Who started nicknames like that — how, why and when — will now never be known but wherever it came from they stuck and Willy was called Willy by everyone at school until the day he left. I even heard one teacher — the cricket coach — use it.

It was different for me: my parents called me Tooks from the beginning.

Willy's parents knew what he was called and hated it. But, to be fair, Willy didn't seem to mind, although now no one calls him that except me and Gregan. Obviously, Lynley — his P.A. — now knows it, as I use it freely when I'm in his office, but she would never use it.

Equally forgotten is exactly how we became and remained friends. We met as boarders at Kings and were (are) almost exactly the same age. But our backgrounds were completely different. As a Morrinsville farmer's son I had more in common with Matamata Gregan, although I despised him then as I do now.

Meanwhile Willy and I became and remained close friends despite having almost nothing in common. As a boy he — Paul Angus Wilbraham — was a fair-dinkum born and bred Remuera city-slicker. Despite the less than salubrious professional premises in Ponsonby Terrace, his father and grandfather had both been eminent and wealthy criminal lawyers there; his grandfather was a K.C.

Unlike me, who resented my father's assumption that I would join him on the farm and eventually inherit the whole estate built up by our ancestors over more than a hundred years, Willy happily followed the trail blazed by his father and grandfather, which inevitably led to a career in law based in the family's Ponsonby chambers. He accepted it as his destiny.

Despite living in Auckland, he boarded at King's because both his grandfather and father had, and they both believed it would 'be the making of the boy'. Unlike me, Willy thrived at school. He eventually became head prefect, had his own fag, and was dux the same year I was expelled. He went on to university, graduating in both commerce and law, before inevitably joining his father in the family firm, replacing his father, who was once the 'Son' and who had joined his own late barrister father in nineteen fifty-six.

That was in nineteen eighty-three. Willy was about to begin his professional career, his training complete, just as I was beginning at art school after two wasted years on the farm and another studying architecture.

The Messenger family of Morrinsville was no less well-bred than the Wilbrahams of Remuera, and much more wealthy, although most of our wealth was locked up in the three hugely productive Waikato dairy farms, the first of which was founded in eighteen ninety. All three were freehold by the time Father took over their management in nineteen seventy-one. Now, together or separately, they're in other, unknown hands.

Father, too, was a King's old boy. He knew of — but didn't know or remember — Willy's father, who was a few years older than he, but he admired the older man for his criminal law reputation, his presidency of the Auckland Club, his standing in Rotary, and the shared belief that boarding his only son — me, his only child after Rosamund's untimely death — at King's would be the making of me, especially as he, Father, had nothing but contempt for our local country high school.

He, too, expected his son — me — to join him in the family's business of farm management and to eventually inherit the whole Messenger estate. But, as I have said, I had no interest in farming or country life. Indeed, I came to think of myself as naturally and thoroughly urban, especially during the school holidays I spent with Willy at his home in Victoria Avenue. But on holidays at home, when I was expected to work long and hard on the farm — Father said the 'business' of farming would come later — I discovered that the lush and rolling green fields of the Waikato, the animals which grazed and shat on them, and the great looming Kaimai range in the distance, were scenes that distressed rather than calmed or inspired me. Indeed, I have spent my entire adult life in big cities — mostly London but New York and Paris too — and only now am looking forward to life in faraway Dunedin.

After all I've been through, even little Auckland seems too big.

Anyway, I did poorly at school in sports and all subjects except art. Only there, in that class with a particularly gifted and insightful master, did I consistently excel, winning, in my final year — the year of Willy's Duxship — the celebrated Jonathan White Senior Art Prize. Having been recently expelled, I was inevitably absent from the school prizegiving.

I stayed there, on Willy's steps, thinking such past thoughts while recovering from the shock of relief. A few suited business-type people, men and women, and a couple of hurrying couriers coming and going, had to step around me contemptuously but I didn't move, or care. Eventually, though, I felt better, restored. Checking my watch, I was surprised to see that it was almost a quarter to ten.

I had to backtrack a bit to get to a bank cash machine. I withdrew a couple of hundred dollars, which I knew I'd need for the day, and saw at once that Lynley was right: the money — all the unbelievably infinite line of zeros of it — was indeed sitting in my account. I stared at the print-out, shocked and amazed, until a bloke behind asked me to hurry up. I moved aside, still staringly studying the flimsy little cash machine receipt, amused to see that my petty withdrawal had made no meaningful difference to the balance.

Even so: eighty-four dollars something for thirty grams of tobacco.

As I've had to be careful about money I'm still finding it hard to get used to New Zealand prices. For everything. Although, to be fair, I know cigarettes and tobacco are heavily taxed as a cost deterrent. I don't like it. Using tax to engineer morals, they call it.

Meanwhile, at the counter, I silently marvelled at the way cigarettes and tobacco are now displayed — or *not* displayed — behind locked doors. I'm old enough to remember when cigarette advertising was everywhere, when even sports teams were sponsored by big tobacco brands, when anyone could afford to smoke and most men did, and you could do it in pubs and restaurants. It was almost compulsory.

Before dropping it into a rubbish bin outside the dairy, I carefully shook the very last of my old tobacco packet's brown, stale and dusty dregs into the freshly bought new packet, pregnantly round, full of fresh and fragrant tobacco, the feel and scent of which immediately relieved the previously extreme but now mild anxiety which arose when I received Lynley's news and returned when I saw the bank receipt.

The round and spongy firm feel of the full tobacco packet in my hand, and then in my pocket, were as satisfying — at least for a few minutes — as having an actual smoke. I noted again, as I had hundreds of times before, the graphic CANCER warnings which took up most of the packet. They didn't deter me, never had, but on this occasion they made me think again of Fiona and Uncle Frank, and of Gregan and his alleged cancer.

If Gregan really does have cancer, then it wasn't caused by smoking — he never smoked — so that proves something, although I don't know what. Anyway, with that unpleasant and unwelcome thought I set off again on the south side of Ponsonby Road, heading for Richmond Road and Davy's.

10.

I DIDN'T HAVE an appointment at Davy's but it didn't matter. I had plenty of time. Davy has two chairs in his little shop but he's the only barber. He was working when I got there, nearly finished on a young bloke who was fussy about which parts of his tattooed head he wanted shaved and which bits of his purple-dyed lank hanks he wanted left long. Davy seemed happy to oblige.

I've noticed that barbers around the world have learned to cheerfully satisfy the weird demands of their young male customers, gladly taking their money while self-censoring their own opinions.

Hair has always been important to young guys. Unlike girls, who have plenty of ways to express themselves as they pass into adulthood — clothes, jewellery, make-up, shoes, and hair — boys are somewhat limited and so use the hair on their head, and on their face if they have any, to make statements about their supposed masculinity, creativity and individuality. They often make poor decisions, happily sporting a ridiculous arrangement of their locks, which they will one day remember with embarrassment, cringing when old photographs are discovered by others. In my young days it was all punk rockers, Doc Martins, ripped jeans with chains and safety pins, screaming unmusical music, and dyed mohawk haircuts. I knew about those things but following such trends was impossible at Kings and, later, utterly impractical for a young farm worker.

In those day, on the farm under Father's supervision, I never had anything more rebellious than long hair — although not even as long as it is now — which was pretty much the norm, anyway. He didn't like it, said having long hair around farm machinery was dangerous. Anyway, I wasn't really interested in punk rock. The art, philosophy and folk music of the 'sixties interested me more. I felt born into the wrong generation.

And so, as the surly, young, tattooed, purpled-haired one left the shop, and the old hairy me took his place in the chair, while Davy briskly swept the freshly-cut and -shaved locks into the corner, I wondered what opinion he, the young barber, might be suppressing about me, my unruly hair and beard.

I needn't have worried; Davy seemed as neutral about my long, wavy and greying mane, and the somewhat coarser wiry beard resting on the black plastic apron he had so skilfully slipped under it, as he had seemed about his previous customer's style. Indeed, as we discussed my requirements — to have both hair and beard only lightly trimmed, with the emphasis on my ending up looking the same only tidier — he seemed to drift into a dream-like state where he worked almost automatically, talking incessantly as he snipped and clipped with scissors that seemed to sing and ring metallically. As a result, I got exactly what I needed hair- and beard-wise from a professional barber while in the process hearing the young man's life story.

Cancer again.

Evidently the Davy Wickham barber shop was founded by Davy's father, also Davy, which is why young Davy could retain the shop's name. Young Davy joined his father after completing his apprenticeship elsewhere — he told me where but I can't remember and it doesn't matter — and they worked together until only two years ago when his father tripped on a step at the back of the shop, going to the outdoor loo for leak, according to the story-teller, and broke his leg. Evidently, it snapped like a dry stick. On examination in hospital it was discovered that old Davy's leg bones were almost eaten away by cancer. I'm not sure if that's right or possible but that's what I was told. Anyway, the poor man was dead within six months.

Mum's okay, said the young and talkative barber, because she now owns the whole building of four shops in a row, flats above. Good rents from me, the other three shops and four flats. And I'm doing okay running the business on my own, he said. Enjoying it, actually. Got a website and everything.

By then he had finished his work on me and had two customers waiting. A mirror check, a stiff brush down, and I was on my way, only a few grams lighter by weight but a full thirty-two dollars lighter by money, including a couple of dollars for a Crunchie bar for Uncle Frank.

I wasn't allowed to wholly leave, though, until Davy and his two waiting customers debated — for my benefit and their enjoyment — the merits of each neighbourhood lunch bar and its pies and doughnuts. The consensus (eventually): The Wakey-Wakey Bakery just up the road past Williamson Avenue. Evidently a good old-fashioned Kiwi bakery where they — Davy and his waiting customers — promised that my sick friend (as I referred to Gregan) and I were certain to be satisfied.

They were right. Gregan was happy. But that was later.

It was only a quarter till eleven when I finished at Davy's so I knew had time to walk to Uncle Frank's in Williamson Avenue. Having thanked Davy and his customers for their advice, I stood outside the shop to roll a cigarette, to smoke as I walked, as I knew smoking was strictly forbidden at Uncle Frank's small, private, luxurious and expensive care home.

It took me just quarter of an hour to get to Uncle Frank's, a big sprawling two-storied mansion on an unusually large site for Ponsonby. It looks like a private home — no doubt it once was — but it's now surrounded by a tall fence with a security gate in the centre (to keep people *in* rather than out). I had to announce myself, as usual. They know me there, so they opened the gate without delay. They always do.

The gate opens to a straight and wide, concrete-edged shelly path bordered on both sides by a low and neatly-trimmed box hedge. The bright green lawns beyond the hedges, spread as flat and smooth as matching bowling greens, are unbroken by trees or garden ornaments, although a narrow border of various shrubs runs along the front of the house, each side of the path and front steps, to soften the clinical and artificial-looking lawns. The path leads directly to a set of steps up to a wide, wooden veranda and a heavy front door flanked by elaborately designed coloured leadlight glass panes.

Matron — her name is Yvonne Something — is a professional charmer, although I can't say the same for her staff.

How is he today? I asked Yvonne when she met me, standing at the front desk. It's the question I always had to ask, as the old man's condition varied by the day and even by the hour, sometimes.

Oh, Mr Messenger, she said with a grimace-cum-amused-smile as she gently and briefly touched a hand to my forearm. His old man's still a dustman.

Oh, no, I said, disappointed but perhaps not surprised.

I had to take away his banjo this morning, she said. He went to his room in a sulk.

Can I see him now? I asked. I've bought him a Crunchie bar.

Oh, he *will* like that, said the matron with an insincere smile.

So, can I see him?

Of course. He's probably settled by now.

Can he have his banjo back?

Perhaps later, she said with a screwed up face which I took to mean 'probably not'. We'll see, she added.

I'll tell him, I said.

I went along to his room and found him sitting on his bed in his blue-and-white striped pyjamas with his arms wrapped around his drawn up legs, a woolly beanie on his scarred, scabby and hairless head, staring at the wall. The television set was on, flickering away soundlessly high in one corner of the room, but he wasn't watching it.

He looked up as I entered, and I waited — just a second — to see if he recognized me. He didn't always but this morning he did. His face brightened up at once and he swung his legs off the bed and searched around the floor with his feet to find his slippers. I noticed that his skinny ankles, on show between his pyjamas and mismatching socks, looked scaly and blotchy.

Sit down, boy, he said, pointing to the shiny, tan-coloured, vinyl-covered armchair beside the bed, the only chair in the room. He wriggled his socked feet into his slippers and sat on the edge of the bed, watching me carefully as I handed him his Crunchie bar — which he took and set down on his side table without comment or thanks — and sat down somewhat below him.

He looked down at me intently. Tonight's the night, isn't it, he said.

I was surprised he remembered, but there's always been so much surprising about Uncle Frank.

Yes, I said. No more than that.

He nodded. Well, good luck, son, he said.

Thanks, I said, and asked him how he was. How he was coping. He said he was all right. Had to go to hospital yesterday, he said.

I knew that but I was surprised he remembered.

They done something, he added. Some medicine or something. Felt crook for a while but I'm over it now mostly. Pissed me off, though. What's the time?

I looked at my watch. Nearly eleven, I said.

Bugger. Still an hour till lunch.

You've been singing again, I said.

Bitch took away my banjo.

You have to stop singing and playing in the corridor, Uncle, I said. Do what you like in the rec room. That's what Yvonne said.

I forget. I keep forgetting.

You haven't forgotten how to sing and play, though.

He laughed at that. Heartily. Had a brief coughing fit. I waited.

Jesus, Tooks, he said when he recovered, we did have fun you know. Back in the day.

Uncle Frank's been a musician all his life. Used to play the banjo — and the clarinet too — in a sort-of Dixieland band.

I didn't really know Uncle Frank when I was growing up as he and his father — my grandfather — had a huge falling out when he refused to work on the farm. That's how my father, Frank's younger brother, came to inherit the farms. I suppose that's why we got on, me and Uncle Frank: we both hated the country — working on the farms — and we both defied our respective fathers.

I hate the country, said Uncle Frank when he and I met again at Father's funeral. When he learned that I was still in London he said, Always loved the city. Love the noise and the people. Love music. Dances. Jazz. Sheilas. Life. Love to go to London. But I *hate* the friggin' country.

Just like me, I thought.

And so, as a young rebellious son, he came to Auckland and got a job driving the trolley buses which were gradually replacing the old trams. Must have been 'fifty-five or -six.

Used to drive the Number Two right down Ponsonby Road, he often said. Did the Richmond Road Three and Herne Bay One routes, too.

Driving the trolley buses and playing in the band: the two things that dominated his frequent reminiscences.

There were just two framed photos on Uncle Frank's side table: a faded colour picture of his band — The Dixie Six — proudly sporting their instruments and posing on a stage somewhere in their white shirts, black waistcoats, red bow ties and red-banded boaters, and a larger black-and-white photo of Uncle Frank alone in his uniform and cap, standing proudly on the street at the front door of a Number Two trolley bus. I always wondered why there was no photo of his wife, my Auntie Joyce, but he never mentioned her so neither did I. She had passed on by the time I came back for Father's funeral. He had retired but was still living alone in his Westmere house, and still playing in some band or other.

Uncle Frank and Auntie Joyce never had any children. I don't know why and never asked. I've never had kids, either. Well, not that I know of. Fiona always said she once wanted to have children — at least one — but by the time we got together she was pretty well past it. Anyway, now I think I've got enough to worry about without kids. In fact, as far as I can see, parents spend their whole lives worrying about their kids and then their grandkids. Not for me.

But back to my Uncle Frank visit.

What are you going to do, boy? he asked. After tonight?

I wondered what he knew about tonight. I asked him.

Only what you told me, he said.

Uncle Frank and I kept in touch after Father's funeral, when I got back to London — by letter at first and then by text messaging once he got the hang of his phone — so he knew about my plans. Indeed, apart from Zelnick and Mrs Barkstone, he and Willy were the only people in New Zealand who knew anything much about me and my plans.

He asked me when he could get his banjo back so I told him what matron had said: Only if you promise not to play and sing in the corridors or dining room.

11.

I TOOK MY time getting to Gregan's. I had a coffee at a new place on Ponsonby Road where I could sit outside and have a quiet smoke before heading up to the Wakey-Wakey place for the pies and doughnuts; I did that last so the pies would still be reasonably hot when I got to Lincoln Street.

All the time I was there with Gregan — watching him greedily tucking into his hot pie, splashing it with more and more tomato sauce, blowing on it to cool it down, and sending flaky bits of pastry floating to the floor, and then munching on his long doughnut so that the cream squished out to be collected, with sugary dust, in his moustache — I couldn't help wishing not only that I wasn't there but that I'd never have to be there again.

Little did I know then how the day would pan out. But — this morning at least — I thought it made sense to stay in Gregan's flat until Uncle Frank didn't need me any more; I couldn't abandon the old man. And that meant I'd have to continue to put up with Gregan. I was resigned to the fact that escaping to my little Saint Clair cottage would have to wait.

I asked Gregan about his health, his cancer and therapy, but he was typically evasive. I asked him again about his diet — whether he should be eating pies and doughnuts, buttery pastry, salty meat and gravy, sugary dough and whipped sweetened cream and jam — but once again he brushed aside my concerns.

Can eat anything, he said. Food's not the problem.

What the problem really is, I don't know. Whatever it is, I'm more convinced than ever that it's not cancer. But — typical narcissist — Gregan likes playing the victim, looking for sympathy.

He didn't ask about tonight so I didn't volunteer anything. He did ask if everything's all right in Clarence Street and once I said everything was fine, the flat's good, I like living there, he didn't ask me anything else. Narcissists aren't interested in uncomplicated people or events; they prefer and seek out worried and anxious people with issues and problems which they'll remember to use to their advantage later. Other people's happy events and successes — even simple contentment — breed envy and resentment in a narcissist. Which is why they have no real friends.

As far as I know I'm now Gregan's only 'friend' and yet I can't wait to be rid of him.

Obviously he's spent his life burning off people he might have called friends, until now, when no one will have anything to do with him except me, and as of this morning, I had no choice. They — any 'friends' he once must have had — all obviously learned what I learned long ago in New York: you have to make a complete break from a narcissist, have nothing to do with them. There's no choice. If you're lucky, you might never hear from them again. But, as I learned to my horror, they don't like being spurned and when you make the break they can become angry, violent and malicious. They'll keep trying to win you back with lies, deceit, flattery and promises they'll never keep because they need you to keep feeding their hungry and insatiable egos.

So, the big lesson after you make the complete break: stay alert. Narcissists rarely forget, forgive, or give up.

This, then, is Anthony (Tony) Redvers Gregan, from toupee to toe a complete narcissist. Always showing off. *Thinks* he's better than everyone at *everything*. Looks down his nose at 'ordinary' people. No conversation if it's not about him. Will always find a clever way to turn any conversation on any subject back to himself. (Me, me, me, me.) Hates being criticized. Moody if he doesn't get his own way. And a complete liar. I've caught him out plenty of times. But he's always got a reason, an explanation, an excuse.

Gregan, a complete loser — with an inherited fortune — who always talks like a winner. Gregan, my age, never done a useful thing in his pathetic life. Gregan, the once disgraced and now unemployable sharebroker. Gregan, the one-time car salesman who was always tooling around in a near-new Mercedes as though it was his and not off the showroom floor. Gregan, the one-time real estate agent who lost his licence for misleading buyers and falsifying legal documents. Gregan, with his young — very young — slutty girlfriends, flash suits, flashy smile, and an intellect as dull as dirt.

I've known a few narcissists in the world — including New York Bernadine — and Gregan isn't the worst, but he's pretty awful and I'll be glad when I'm finally in Saint Clair, so far away.

I was with him today, at lunch, for much longer than I'd planned, longer than I wanted, but he didn't want me to leave and insisted on opening an expensive bottle of wine.

Marlborough, private bin, very expensive, he said. I know the winemaker personally. Bloody good bloke. Known him for years. And his husband if you get my meaning.

I'm not an alcoholic but I know I might have been, could have been. In that dark New York year, with Bernadine, I nearly was. But I gave up drinking, with all the other stuff, years ago and haven't had a drop since.

After today I suspect Gregan's an alcoholic which means unless he does something about it — stop drinking, I mean — he's doomed. I've known a few alcoholics and they were all doomed. To die, I mean. And horribly. I learned that in London: unless they reform — stop drinking altogether and forever — all alcoholics are doomed.

So I declined to join Gregan in his lunchtime habit, despite his almost rude insistence, but stayed a while to be polite while he drank alone. I had a smoke while he drank — weirdly for a cancer patient he didn't mind my smoking but simply continued drinking until the bottle was empty and he was drunk.

I had wondered why he so much wanted me to be there today, what he wanted from me — narcissists *always* have an ulterior motive — but as I sat there smoking, listening to his increasingly drink-fuelled talk, I realized that, on this occasion at least, he wanted no more than company and a listening ear. I saw that with nothing to do, nowhere to go, no friends, the bottle had become his only companion, his only solace. I suspect that drinking to inebriation at lunchtime is a daily habit.

Yes, an alcoholic.

Like all drunks, Gregan's rambling monologue — it was an entirely one-sided conversation — contained frequent over-confident and slurred assertions that 'You're a really good guy', 'I've always admired you', 'It's *not* the drink talking, mate', 'This is just between you and me, okay?', 'I mean it, I really do', 'I haven't told anyone else', 'Mates since school,' and, of course, 'We trust each other, right? Always have. Always will.'

As a result of his unbridled talking and my reluctant listening, I realized that Gregan only *feared* he had cancer. Certain friends, he said, had died recently following symptoms, headaches, similar to those he was experiencing. It's our age, isn't it, he stated. You'll see. At sixty the wheels start falling off. All sorts of things go wrong. I've noticed that, haven't you? he slurred.

Had he been to a doctor? No, he said. Too bloody scared.

I left Gregan's a bit after two when his talking stopped and he became drowsy. I realized then that he hadn't thanked me for his pie and doughnut, which annoyed me a bit but I should have known better.

Anyway, on the walk back up to Ponsonby Road I felt pretty depressed. I couldn't help thinking about both alcoholism and cancer.

Cancer's not something I'd ever thought about before but since Fiona I've thought about it a lot. And now Gregan and his almost certainly *not* cancer.

But he was right in a way: by the time we get to sixty — if we do get to sixty, many don't — we can sense our bodies getting tired and think we can see the end of the road.

After knowing many people — friends and acquaintances — who have died of cancer, and then seeing Fiona through everything till the end, all through London's ridiculous covid lockdowns and on-again/off-again rules, I came to the conclusion that pretty much everything we know about cancer, everything we've been told by the experts — the doctors and scientists — including their recommended treatments and therapies, is wrong.

I came to the conclusion that cancer's *not* a disease. It's not the result of a germ or virus or something invading the body and attacking its vital organs. On the contrary; far from being sick, weak and failing, cancer cells are healthy, strong and vigorous. Indeed, the therapies used to treat this so-called 'disease' are especially designed to kill cells that may indeed be 'rogue' but are in fact exceedingly healthy. No other medication or therapy is designed to literally kill healthy cells, and how can lethal chemicals or radiation ever really know the difference between healthy normal cells and *very* healthy cancer cells?

It seems to me that to dream of 'curing' cancer is futile, as futile as believing that death is a disease that can be cured. Furthermore, if cancer really were to be cured — if, somehow, it was miraculously eradicated — then it would merely be replaced by something worse simply because we all have to die of something. Eventually I decided that getting cancer is just another name for dying slowly.

My guess is that the real cause of cancer will never be found because there is no single or identifiable 'cause'. It's just *life*. It seems that the cells of the body's organs somehow sense or are told that time's up for their host body. As a result, some cells decide that they can stop slavishly reproducing as, say, liver cells, or pancreas cells, or any special-purpose cells, and just be *cells*; non-specific. It's as if nature says, This bloke will be dead soon, it'll all be over, so you might as well go ahead and do your own thing.

The bases for nature's decision must be many, varied and largely unknown. Perhaps nature calculates how much animal fat or sugar or salt or alcohol or smoke or sun or exercise (or anything) the human body should naturally and normally be exposed to in a lifetime. And so, when that limit is reached, the cells of the body might reasonably assume that their host's body is nearing the end of its life, thus giving them licence to abandon their duties and so become 'rogue'.

I've mentioned my theory to doctors, who just think I'm bloody stupid, but I think it's a fair argument. However, I've never been able to reconcile it with cancer in children, who have obviously not lived long enough to reach any of nature's warning limits. I can only assume that either the stricken children have some underlying but unknown condition or that their cells really *have* gone uncontrollably 'rogue'.

But what, I always wondered, did fifty-nine-year-old Fiona Christina Gallacher do or consume to excess that meant her pancreas cells stopped doing their duty? As for eighty-eight-year-old Uncle Frank, at his age it could have been anything. He smoked once but the problem was in his brain. Sometimes, I think, without either a disease or a failing heart, the body just gets too old and so gives up and surrenders to cancer; the inevitable.

Who the hell knows?

12.

BACK ON PONSONBY Road — and thoroughly depressed by Gregan, his drinking, his cowardly fear of his imagined cancer, and the very real cancer that took Fiona and will no doubt (I thought then) take Uncle Frank — I sat at a bus stop to, ironically, relax with another smoke; a bus had just left so there was no one there to object.

And there, across the road, upstairs, as if to remind me of my age and my depressing thoughts of growing old, cancer and dying: 'The Ponsonby Powerhouse' with its floor-to-ceiling windows, and the obviously young men and women in tight and luridly-coloured clothes bought especially for use only at that place or places like it. There they were, on a Friday afternoon, not working at a job but 'working out' as they call it: running on a treadmill, pulling weights through pulleys or otherwise pushing or pulling or heaving against artificially-created resistance, using their arms, legs or back, in an unconscious imitation of *real* hard, physical, back-breaking, sweat-inducing work that *real* workers were no doubt doing not for fun but for a living, this fine Friday afternoon in autumn, in factories, on machines, on ships and wharves, building sites, roads and quarries.

Such exercise places — gyms — always remind me of George Orwell's *The Road to Wigan Pier.* I remember how Orwell always, in his research and writing, showed respect for England's exploited working class, the dignity of work and all that. He talked about how hard work — but not too much — never hurt anyone. He was referring to the hard-working but underpaid and exploited coal miners and mill workers he saw and heard, their clogs clacking on the cobbles on their way to and from the pit or mill, in the dark, morning and night. Indeed, as I recall, he praised and respected them for their work ethic while condemning the capitalist industrial system that exploited their willingness and ability to work hard for their families' survival by overworking them and underpaying them.

What impressed me was that he speculated then, in the nineteen thirties, that the advance of mechanization and automation — he was referring to the automation of machinery at a time before computers were even dreamed of — meant the coming of a time when manual workers would be utterly redundant and that their health would therefore fail as a result of their new sedentary lifestyle and lack of exercise.

He speculated then that governments would have to establish special places fitted with cleverly designed exercise machines on which the unfit and unmuscular men — their hard work then being done by machines — would have to exercise in a manner designed to replicate the hard work of earlier generations in order to attain and maintain good health.

Orwell was right. He was right in his desire to elevate respect for hard work and Britain's working class. He was right to see that physical exercise was essential to bodily health. And he was also right to see that beyond a healthy level of physical work came exploitation and the opposite of good health: men made to work like horses, broken and exhausted in only their middle years, dying young of exhaustion, malnourishment and disease.

And there, across Ponsonby Road, on the upper floor like a stage, behind floor-to-ceiling windows there to be seen through, I saw prophetic Orwell's exercise machines being used, at great expense, in the futile pursuit of guaranteed good health, good looks and eternal youth in the defiance of unstoppable time.

Vanity.

I wanted to rush upstairs there and then and tell them all — furiously and sweatingly pushing, pulling, running and heaving — what

I believe: that they (and we all) have been given a fixed number breaths, a fixed number of heartbeats, a fixed number of days to live, and while we can easily reduce those numbers — by foolishness or accident — there is nothing we can do to increase them.

And, I wanted to add, despite your frenetic exercising in the interests of being and looking beautiful and handsome and healthy, if you do continue to survive you *will* undoubtedly age. Nothing is more certain. Despite your exercises and your vanity, your muscles *will* shrivel, your skin *will* sag and wrinkle, your bones *will* become brittle, and if your various and vital organs don't actually become diseased they will weaken, function less efficiently until they eventually fail. And then, if nothing else happens, your heart will eventually stop. That I promise. *Guarantee.* And then you will die and the body you were so proud of, which you fed only the purest, most expensive and natural organic food, which you exercised so rigorously and religiously and paraded in front of others with unseemly pride, will be returned to the earth from which it came.

Nature has nothing but contempt for human vanity.

Indeed, at my age I realize — can actually see — that everyone I know, everyone I meet, everyone around me who is past adolescence, is already dying. Slowly but surely dying.

That is our destiny.

This, then, was the depressing nature of my ongoing contemplation as I sat alone, smoking, in that Ponsonby Road bus stop shelter. Someone — a young guy, a student, I think — shrugged off his back-pack and sat on the bench along from me, his pack on the pavement between his feet, and scowled at me superciliously before staring down at his phone and flicking the screen with his thumb. His arrival and scowl broke my melancholy. I got his message and flicked my butt into the street. I'd finished it, anyway. And then a couple of other people arrived and stood looking up at the flickering timetable sign and down the street expectantly; evidently a bus was due. Their presence forced me to return my thoughts to the depressing here-and-now reality, the empty afternoon ahead — I looked at my watch: not even half-past-two — and the mystery of Number Twelve.

Suddenly, my phone Pink Floyded again, so I stood up and moved away from the little bunch of bus-stop-waiting people and began walking aimlessly up towards K Road.

It was Yvonne Something, the usually professionally pleasant matron at Uncle Frank's place in Williamson Avenue. But she didn't sound so pleasant on this occasion. She was sorry to trouble me — she sounded stern and not at all sorry — you must be so busy and everything, but your uncle—

The long and the short of it was that Uncle Frank had sneaked into the office, retrieved his banjo, and gone into a Mrs Barlow's room to serenade her with his favourite song, 'My Old Man's a Dustman'. (Yes, I too had to look it up.) Evidently the bedridden Mrs Barlow was asleep and was so shocked by Uncle Frank's musical invasion of her room, privacy and sleep, that she had to be treated by the doctor and was now in a sedative-induced daze. Meanwhile Uncle Frank had to be restrained — My goodness, he's still so strong, said Yvonne — and was now lying in his locked room, sedated like Mrs Barlow, his banjo permanently confiscated.

But he was so good this morning, I protested.

Yvonne agreed. He *was* good this morning, she said, but after you left, well, I'm afraid he's about as bad as he's ever been. It's the tumour, you see, pressing and acting on his brain. That's what the doctor said, anyway.

Poor Uncle Frank, I thought. Drugged and locked up like an animal, or a prisoner.

I asked her what she wanted me to do.

There's nothing to be done, Mr Messenger, she said. We just thought you ought to know. Actually, she added, we're *required* to inform you.

I'll try and call in later, I said.

That was my plan but it didn't work out like that.

Sitting here now, late at night, at the end of what turned out to be a pretty eventful day, I can see that what happened was inevitable. But standing there this afternoon, in the middle of the Ponsonby Road footpath, listening to Yvonne Something, the matron, on the phone, as annoyed people nudged me, scowled at me, stepped around me as they hurried along on their business, I had no idea how it would all end. Not just Uncle Frank but everything, the whole day.

Eventually, inevitably, I *did* discover what was 'wrong' with Number Twelve — what was missing — although what I thought was the problem and what that Lallemand person thought were entirely different. And while all that was happening — the confrontation with the Lallemand man at Zelnick's — Uncle Frank passed away peacefully in his drug-induced sleep.

I didn't know *that* was coming when I spoke to matron Yvonne this afternoon. I asked if I should come and see him but she said there was no point, that he was out cold — she didn't say that exactly but that's what she meant — and would stay that way until at least early evening, when Doctor Goldson would be in to check on him. What he'll be like when he wakes up, she said, she had no idea.

We won't know anything until then, she said.

I said I'd pop in later. I thought it would be pretty late. Could be nine o'clock or so. She said it would only be night staff then but it should be all right. I'll tell Jo-Anne to expect you, she said. To let you in.

But I never got there. Never met Jo-Anne. Never saw Uncle Frank. In fact I'll never see him alive again.

13.

THREE O'CLOCK. I caught a taxi up to Zelnick's. I knew he'd be there, all frowning and anxious and making ready.

The exhibition gallery was closed, of course, but there were a few people idly looking around the main hall. Mrs Barkstone was looking after a client. They were together, standing back from a typically large, lumpy and bumpy Braithwaite, clearly discussing not the merits of the obviously early and valuable work — probably late 'sixties I thought — but the price.

Fiona and I met Blanche Braithwaite once, in Manchester, at an exhibition. Such a very interesting woman. She was getting on a bit then but still pretty lively. I found her husband to be a bit hard going but Fiona said he was an alcoholic; had been for years. I saw later, in *The Times*, that he had died. He was a lot older than her but pretty well known in his own way.

I assume she's still alive. She's pretty famous in England, although Fiona said Chetwin-Lewis — father *and* son — had no time for her.

Wouldn't touch her stuff. Don't know why. Anyway, I'm sure I would have heard if she'd died.

Mrs Barkstone saw me come in. Without interrupting the discussion about the Braithwaite, without her customer even noticing, she used her eyes, and a tiny movement of her head, to tell me that Mort was in his office at the back of the building.

The little man, always impeccably dressed and groomed, and even now, in his seventies, bright and sprightly, looked up frowningly and almost jumped from his chair to come around his desk to greet me.

Ah, my good friend, he said soberly, still frowning with apparent worry, as he took and shook my hand — he always does — the heavy gold bracelet on his wrist and the jewelled rings on his fingers flashing in the afternoon sunlight.

Despite his gallery being windowless, its works being lit with carefully and cleverly arranged artificial lighting, Zelnick insisted on inspecting everything in the natural light of his spacious, west-facing, well-windowed office.

Having shaken my hand, he stepped back, lifted his right hand in the air with a flourish.

I have found, he said, with— he then lowered his hand and pointed his first two fingers close to his eyes —my own eyes, a problem with the

Number Twelve. Something important, no? is very missing.

What! My intuition was right. But what, I wondered, was the problem? What on earth could be missing?

Come, you must see, said Zelnick. Before tonight when the peoples arrive. He glanced at his heavy and ostentatious gold watch. Is only a few hours, no? he said. Come. Come.

And so I followed the eccentric little man — somewhat famous for his heeled boots, flashy suits, and love of golden jewellery — through the kitchen, where a maroon-aproned catering couple were laying out the food platters for 'the peoples' expected later. And there, in the hushed, unlit and gloomy exhibition room, I saw my Twelve hanging together for the first time. They were all the same size, long, unstretched canvasses fixed to aluminium battens at the top and bottom but fraying naturally at the sides.

Zelnick will show your great missing mistake, said the gallery owner and dealer as he flicked on a row of switches to light the whole gallery softly and each painting brightly. There were four paintings on each of three walls.

Come, he said, as he walked briskly to the last painting on the wall to our right. There, he said, presenting Number Twelve somewhat triumphantly. Zelnick presents your mistake.

I looked but saw nothing wrong. In fact it was the last of the series and so, I thought, the best.

Mort, I'm sorry, but I don't see. Show me.

How can I show something that's not there? Is impossible.

With that he wheeled around on his left heel, his hand sweeping the room theatrically.

Is Zelnick stupid or blind as a brat or what have you? he asked rhetorically. Look, numbers One to Eleven, there, in the corner, your big 'T' and little slash twenty-four little slash number. Clear as daytime is it. But here, the Number Twelve. Nothing, zero, zilch, gornisht, nichts.

Suddenly I realized it. Saw what wasn't there, what was missing. Number Twelve. It wasn't signed. That's what my doubts had been about. Somehow — unbelievably — I'd forgotten to sign it.

Oh dear, I said weakly.

Ahhh, said Zelnick, leaning forward, drooping his head and flopping his arms limply to his sides as if exhausted by what it took to show me the obvious. At last you see it what Zelnick has not seen all the times.

Actually I was somewhat relieved to have discovered the somewhat minor source of my intuitive doubts, something so trivial and easily fixed.

It doesn't matter, Mort, I said. I've signed the back with my name as well as my 'T' the date and the number. That's all it needs. And, anyway, it's too late now. The paint would never dry in time for tonight. I'll do it later.

But the buyers? The clients? The collectors? They are Zelnick's personal invitations. They come soon with money. What will they say? What will they think of Zelnick and his protégé? Not even to sign his painting already?

I ignored Zelnick's protestations then and took the time to slowly absorb the look and feel of the room. The walls and ceiling were painted matt white, the floor was polished concrete, three soft couches were set in the middle of the room, each facing one of the exhibition walls, and a long table draped with a white linen cloth — awaiting the evening's refreshments — stood against the only blank wall, into which was set the door from the main hall. I thought my Twelve looked especially fine in that environment, as good an exhibition as I've ever had anywhere in the world.

I told the silly old bugger it didn't matter, said Mrs Barkstone, who was suddenly at my side.

I smiled down at the dark lady whose role in Zelnick's life and business was a mystery to me.

If it sells, I said — Oh, it'll sell, Mr Messenger, she interrupted. It'll definitely sell

— Well, I continued, if it sells tonight we'll see what the new owner wants.

Of this I am not so sure of it, said Zelnick with a slow and scowling head shake.

Silly old bugger, said Mrs Barkstone, not quietly.

I said it all looked wonderful and thanked them both.

Be here at seven, said the lady. Actually, a little after.

I'll be here.

It's going to be a big success, she said. A big success.

This is what we be always hoping, said Zelnick.

Mrs Barkstone offered me a cup of tea but I was busting for a smoke so I declined and instead walked up Parnell Road and sat on the grass under a tree at the side of the cathedral.

Holy Trinty. Everything about this cathedral is hugely impressive especially the huge expanse of stained glass at the back of the nave that features a Māori Jesus. As a religious building it cleverly evokes and combines both traditional Polynesian buildings and English colonial church architecture. I've seen its Polynesian inspiration in much simpler buildings all over the Pacific, including Hawaii, new Caledonia and Tahiti, while its traditional heritage — the old and small wooden cathedral which it replaced — still stands, looking somewhat dowdy and humiliated in its shadow.

I was smoking so I didn't go inside the cathedral. But I've been there many times recently as well as when I was a long-ago student of both architecture and art. In fact the late Robert Ellis, one of my professors at art school, designed some of the stained glass windows along the side of the nave.

It is, without question, a beautiful and very impressive building of architectural integrity. But as I sat there this afternoon, smoking and day dreaming, I couldn't help thinking again about the vast but empty cathedrals of England and Europe, and that, like them, this modern iteration is not much more than a comforting symbol of a time when Christianity was at the centre of our civilization.

As I finished my smoke and stood up to move on, it occurred to me for the first time that no church, of any age, style or size, is represented in my Twelve, now hanging in the dark at Zelnick's gallery down Parnell Road. And that reminded me that something about Number Twelve was still bothering me. I know *now* what the *real* problem was but at the time — this afternoon — I realized I wasn't entirely satisfied with Zelnick's discovery of the missing signature.

I admit it was odd that not only had I forgotten to add my new 'T' signature, so much like a 'J' anyway, to the last and best of the series — I had practised it often enough and had added it to the other eleven as they were finished — but also that I hadn't even noticed its absence until it was pointed out by Zelnick. But my reliable intuition — it has never let me down — was telling me that something was *still* not quite right with Number Twelve. I didn't know what it was, although I found out later.

14.

WITH NOTHING ELSE to do I decided to walk to the domain, where I knew I could sit on the steps of the museum, away from the Parnell traffic, and look across the park and the trees to the city beyond. It was the contrast I loved, the theme of so much of my work. The soft roundness and muted colours of nature's shrubbery — still green today but only just — with the vertical and sharp angularity of the city's tall and modern buildings behind, all new and shiny, metallic and glassy, and the slender Sky Tower looking as sleek and sharp and nasty as an upright syringe. It was that dramatic contrast — between man's work and nature's — I saw and painted in London, New York and Paris and so tried to capture again in Auckland in The Twelve.

I felt like a cigarette but it felt sacrilegious to smoke there, on the steps of that great museum dedicated to the war dead. The view was so grand, so evocative, that I decided to wait.

They're not all good, these modern city business buildings, not all well designed, not always (or hardly ever) in good taste, and not necessarily even well built. Indeed, how long will they last? As long as the Tower of London? Windsor Castle? Westminster Abbey? the Pantheon, the Parthenon? Stonehenge? The pyramids of Egypt and America?

And what do they stand for?

Although I've admired them and painted them all my life, all over the world, it's a question I've never been able to answer. I've never really understood what they literally stand for. Is it really necessary to raise a building thirty, eighty, a hundred or more stories? Storey stacked above storey housing hundreds of businesses employing thousands of people spending the precious hours of their short lives doing what?

In the ancient and even recent past we raised huge buildings to honour our gods and remind us of our insignificance, dwarfed beside their monumental height and bulk. Now we raise these so-called skyscrapers to honour what? The gods of money and profit? In the process they — these great houses of commerce — serve to remind us, purposely or incidentally, of the insignificance of our brief existence. They are, to me, taken together — these tall, slender but monumental concrete, steel, aluminium and glassy buildings, crowded together in the centre of any big city — merely the bold and shameless expression of capitalism. I don't like them, I don't even like going up into them, but they fascinate me as physical objects, subjects worth painting, especially when set before or behind the softness, greenness and eternal beauty of nature.

Across the long but narrow harbour, beyond the myriad but fading blue-green tones of the domain and the city's commercial buildings, I could see Stanley Point on the North Shore. It was from the depths of that silvery water, which split the city and which this afternoon looked so steely still and peaceful, that the young Rangitoto burst up with fiery volcanic fury only eight hundred years ago. Although it was hidden from my vantage point this afternoon by a vast, spreading and ancient pōhutukawa, I knew Rangitoto was there, ever present, lying quiet and blue-green, broodingly, in its bath of cool harbour waters.

The vision of this clean and fresh panorama of Auckland had haunted me during the last few years in dirty, scruffy London. I tried to convey it to Fiona in the hope that she might one day return with me. She said she would but, sadly, it was not to be.

It was there, this afternoon, sitting on the broad concrete steps of the museum, warmed by the afternoon autumn sun, that I realized — *really* understood — how lucky I am, how lucky we are, here in this little country. Surely no place on Earth is so distant from the woes and worries of the world. And yet, foolishly, we are as angry, divided, fretful, worried and afraid as anyone anywhere.

But why?

At the moment our current fear — a mass anxiety — is global warming and climate change.

So, what's new? Finding something to fear about the future seems to be part of being human. History tells us that our ancestors, whoever and wherever they were, *always* lived in fear of something, with or without reason. The fear of wild animals, cruel and ruthless invaders, war, crime, volcanoes, earthquakes, floods, drought, poverty, famine or disease, have caused entire civilizations to live in a constant state of fretful apprehension.

Perhaps they were right to be worried about the unknowable future. But if they were wrong, if their particular fear never eventuated, then their entire lives were unnecessarily blighted by anxiety.

So, are we spoiling *our* present by worrying too much and unnecessarily about climate change? There are plenty of much worse things to worry about and yet we innocently and unquestioningly believe the prophesies of the climate 'experts'. They refer to their records to show that this month, season, year, decade or century is the hottest, coldest, wettest, driest or stormiest on record. And things, they say, will only get worse.

What they *don't* say is that their records go back no more than a pathetic hundred-or-so years, while a few thousand years of history is full of *natural-occurring* periods of extreme and unusual heat and cold, flood and drought, storms, volcanoes, earthquakes and tsunamis. Surely nothing can happen climate-wise that hasn't happened before, perhaps many times and probably worse.

And in the *ancient* past — before human existence or influence — there were vast changes in the Earth's climate and at least five mass extinctions, millions of years apart, when changes to the Earth's environment were so dramatic — so catastrophic — that almost all life was destroyed.

It makes a mockery of the records and projections of the 'experts'.

I know I'm pretty much alone in seeing the whole issue as a form of unthinking mass hysteria, so I don't usually say this stuff out loud. I've discussed it in the past and been called a 'silly old prick' so why should I invite that sort of contempt.

How can you think like that, they say, when all the scientists in the world agree?

To unthinkingly believe that scientists are *always* right — have never been wrong — defies history and seems especially naïve. And that 'all the scientists in the world agree' sounds simply improbable.

But, anyway, the question remains: is the climate changing? Probably, because it always has and always will. Can we do anything about it? Probably not. Is the Earth doomed? Well, it was here, in various extreme climatic states, for billions of years even before we existed and it will certainly continue to survive for billions more years, with or without us. It certainly isn't 'doomed'. It certainly doesn't need 'saving'.

Meanwhile, it seems we *need* to fear something about the unknowable future. Today it's global warming and climate change. Tomorrow it'll be something else. Who knows what that will be?

At least there'll be plenty of choice.

15.

THE DESIRE FOR another smoke roused me from my reverie.

I suddenly became aware that the still softly warm sun — the driver of Earth's climate and the source of all life — was nevertheless falling away to the west. It was getting late so I changed my idea about walking home. Instead I turned to take a last look at the great museum behind me, a grand building dedicated not to a god of any kind — not even to the god of money — but to the sacred memory of the men and women of my hometown who lost their lives in war.

I generally object to the glorification of war but cannot object to such an imposing, tasteful and well-built memorial to so many of its innocent victims.

I walked down the hill to the duck pond where I sat on a bench, in the shade, rolled and smoked a cigarette, watched two floating geese doing absolutely nothing — but beautifully — and wondered vaguely about Number Twelve, before walking slowly through the lovely and tranquil domain out to the hospital main gate where I knew I would find a taxi.

The ride home with a talkative lady taxi driver gave me more food for thought to add to my increasingly grumpy and negative mood about the state of the world and its people. My instinctive dislike of electric scooters taking over the city's roads and footpaths was reinforced by the taxi driver's cogent argument against Uber. She told me, in no uncertain terms, almost angrily, that unlike the heavily and strictly regulated taxi industry — regulated for the safety and benefit of its passengers — Uber drivers require no special license or insurance, nor is there any test of their road knowledge nor any regulation concerning the size, age, condition, cleanliness, or general fitness of their car. Nor are their fares regulated; they can charge whatever they like.

And they do.

Same as that bloody Airbnb, she said angrily. Imagine, she said, the rules and regulations imposed on proper hotels and motels.

She said she knew all about it because her brother has a motel up north. Fire safety and insurance alone. And hygiene, ventilation and heating. All designed to protect their guests.

But those bloody Airbnb people, she said. Nothing. Do what they like. Charge what they like. Some are okay, she added as she calmed down. We were nearly home. But some are dreadful. I know. I take people to them. Help them with their bags. No official oversight. It's free enterprise and capitalism gone mad.

Scooters, too, I said, sharing her indignation.

Same as, she said. Exactly. And it all happened under a Labour government. I always vote Labour. They usually like regulation and control. They're there to look after ordinary people like us, aren't they. But they let all this happen. Drives me bloody crazy, excuse my French.

Wow, I thought, a bit taken aback by her vehemence. But I thought she was right. This morning I couldn't explain why those electric scooters annoy me so much. Now I know, thanks to that angry taxi lady.

But will anything happen? I doubt it.

Gordon barked a friendly greeting over the fence as I arrived home. Jaws was waiting on the step, looking up at the door handle. As I found my keys and opened the door he pressed his side against my leg, and looked up pleadingly, showing me his open pink mouth and his rows of sharp little bright white teeth in a silent meow. When the door opened, he squeezed past me, sped to the kitchen, slipping on the vinyl, and stood at his empty dish, waiting expectantly.

Jaws is *always* hungry and never declines food. According to the vet it's possible — probable — that having been a stray, perhaps abandoned as a kitten, or mistreated, he retains some memory of being starving. Also, according to the vet, cats will eat to cope with psychological issues — like boredom, loneliness, grief or depression — just as their owners do. But right now, as I sit here in the gloom, writing under a desk light, he looks thoroughly content, his little stomach full, sleeping soundly in the dark on his own cushion.

Anyway, after getting home this afternoon I had a couple of hours before Zelnick's and although I should have been hungry I wasn't. Between the pie and doughnut at Gregan's, worrying about poor old banjo-less Uncle Frank being locked in his room and, not least, the persistent doubt about Number Twelve and the vague but familiar pre-show nerves, I had no appetite. In fact, the more I thought about eating the more uneasy I felt until, having opened a packet of nauseating cat food, and spooning it into Jaws's dish, I actually sensed the taste of pre-vomit sourness and so threw up into the toilet. Tired and sweating, but relieved, I sat down at my little kitchen table with my precious cowboy boot lighter and new packet of sweet, fresh tobacco from which I drew my Zig Zag papers. However, once the cigarette was burning, having taken a long draw, I felt lightheaded — lack of nourishment, vomiting, smoke — so I moved and slumped into my only armchair, where Jaws is sleeping now, and promptly fell asleep.

I must have slept for only a few minutes. Luckily, as smokers will know, hand-rolled cigarettes, especially when they're thin, need the smoker's constant attention to stay alight. I awoke with a fright and found my cigarette — black and brown and ashy at one end, still wet at the other, on the vinyl floor to my right, where it must have landed and died, having fallen from the relaxed hold of my fingers.

I retrieved it then, and relit it, determined not to fall asleep again. I decided that, no matter what, I should eat something. Zelnick will have nothing more than dainty snacks and wine and, anyway, I rarely get the chance to eat on such occasions. I usually spend the whole time standing about small-talking and holding a glass of warm fruit juice which I barely have the chance to sip.

Meanwhile, and annoyingly, the matter of Number Twelve kept haunting me. Despite Zelnick's discovery of the missing signature I was not convinced that that alone was the problem. Something, I knew, was somehow wrong with Number Twelve. Something else was missing.

Two slices of thick white bread from the freezer, toasted an even brown and spread with butter — melting and dripping — and Vegemite, and a cup of Earl Grey, scalding hot and black, might not have been the ideal well-balanced and nutritious evening meal but it was the perfect way to launch myself out into an autumn night in Parnell to meet the public and press at *The Zelnick Gallery. M. Zelnick proprietor. Founded 1986.*

Mrs Barkstone had given me a printed list of Zelnick's VIP guests but, having been away for so long, the names meant nothing to me. Looking at it now, though, one stands out, never to be forgotten. She'd also advised me, verbally and unnecessarily, about my appearance. She said they'd expect me to look a bit like an artist, adding, but not too much.

Main thing is they're spending a lot of money, so they want you to look at least clean, tidy and respectable, she said.

I checked the kitchen mirror on the way out. After a hot shower and a shampoo of my freshly trimmed hair and beard, I thought I looked a bit like a clean, tidy and reasonably respectable artist.

16.

I ARRIVED AT Zelnick's about quarter after seven.

You must be little late, small bit, Zelnick had said. Make an entry and everybodies will give you clap.

That made me smile but I got the point and, yes, the gallery was full when I arrived and they all — the invited guests — clapped lightly and politely on cue, prompted, no doubt, by Zelnick himself and Mrs Barkstone. Mrs Barkstone led me at once to the bar, where I declined a cold chardonnay but accepted a room-temperature fruit juice, and was immediately introduced, before I could take a sip, to some no doubt wealthy and certainly overweight matron who ooohed and aaahed about something which I can't remember, probably because it was unworthy of the mental effort. I knew I'd have to make a small speech and I wished Zelnick would get on with it, the 'official' opening of the exhibition. Meanwhile, I half-listened to my actually, as I discovered, quite knowledgeable companion — she knew plenty about my Julius work and reputation — as I surreptitiously took in the whole room and noticed that on the wall, bottom right, beside each of The Twelve, was a small but unmissable bright-red sticker.

No wonder Zelnick was being so jolly.

Before long he — Zelnick — stood on a small platform set beside the bar and, looking so dark and small and exotic in his navy-blue pinstripe suit, pale primrose shirt and pink tie, his thick and coarse steely-grey hair slicked back, the gold and gems of his rings, bracelets and tie pin, and his heavy watch, flashing in the ambient light, made a short speech welcoming his 'guests' and (re)introducing me.

So very, very famous in Europe and America, he said, as we all know it, is come home to bring his beautiful work tonight to Zelnick's own gallery. A very, very special occasion for Zelnick and New Zealand and everybodies.

He said a few other things in his unique fashion, including his unoriginal observation — already set out in the small catalogue and otherwise well known and understood — that I have always been fascinated by the contrast between the stiff rigidity, sharp angles and insipid colours of modern buildings, which I render in acrylics, and the yielding softness and myriad colours of nature, for which I use oils.

He also explained — in unnecessary detail, I thought — what was also in the little catalogue: that each of The Twelve paintings in the series represented a month, starting in April, Number One, and ending in March, Number Twelve, the financial year, which governs what he called 'the businesses peoples' occupying the buildings rather than the calendar year, which governs the lives of what he called 'the ordinary peoples', or the seasons which rule over nature.

I said a few words in response from the floor; I didn't need Zelnick's little platform. I can't remember what I said, I had nothing prepared, but whatever it was, by way of thanks, it seemed to satisfy the guests. However, I felt a bit of a fraud simply because I didn't tell my indulgent and attentive audience the real reason I came home. I referred loosely to my 'Julius' career in London, Paris and New York, of course — most of the listeners seemed to know that much about me — but skipped over my Chetwin-Lewis experience, since Willoughby's crimes were not widely known.

I didn't mention Fiona at all, her influence on me, how she saved me from myself, our lives together, what her loss meant and why I was compelled to come home. I couldn't manage it — it seemed too personal — and assumed that if some of the details were known here, then people were probably being considerate. Are my countrymen so kind? Nor did I mention that I was planning to move to Dunedin to be on my own, to escape the world, and that, depending on how I felt there, how the future unfolded, this may or may not be my last exhibition.

I thought Zelnick's VIP guests deserved better but I couldn't bring myself to say anything personal and so I must have sounded somewhat insincere — even bored and detached — which was unfair when I knew that twelve of the people listening had each committed to paying me — via Zelnick — many thousands of dollars.

If I did sound offhand and churlish it didn't seem to matter to the audience, who clapped again, more enthusiastically this time, before turning their attention to the paintings to resee them in the light of Zelnick's over-enthusiastic interpretations and my own brief remarks.

Mrs Barkstone was beginning to tell me how well it was all going, and evidently how quickly everything had sold, when she was interrupted by a pleasant-looking young woman — late thirties I thought — who begged to be introduced.

Oh, I am sorry, said Mrs Barkstone, who obviously knew the young woman. This is Mrs Lallemand, she said, a dedicated collector of New Zealand art and, yes, tonight, one of your lucky buyers.

We shook hands, this bright-eyed and intelligent-looking young woman and I. She didn't have a drink but did have an obviously expensive-brand handbag.

Call me Trish, she said. Please.

Tooks, I said although she called me, and continued to call me, Mr Messenger.

Meanwhile, Mrs Barkstone had managed to slip away.

So which—?

I had to ask the question, and Mrs Lallemand — Trish — was only too happy, anxious even, to answer.

Oh, Number Twelve, of course, she said. And before I could say anything she rushed on excitedly. Oh, it's so wonderful, Mr Messenger, she said. Come and look.

She took my elbow and together we weaved our way through the crowd until we were standing in front of my — now her — Number Twelve.

You see, my husband, she said, David, he'll be here soon — she glanced at her expensive-looking watch — he should be here by now, actually. Well, we've just bought a beautiful house, you see, a mansion, really, if I may say so, in Takapuna. Such a lovely street of pōhutukawas. And so much wall space for all my wonderful pictures. You see, the people who used to live there — not the people we bought it from but the people before that, you understand — well they were, or the lady was I think, famous art collectors, you know. Had everything. Such a marvellous collection. And, well, what I'm trying to say is that your wonderful big painting here, Number Twelve, is going to hang high in the entrance hall, flooded with natural light, where the other people had a dark and threatening McCahon. I know they did because I saw it in an old copy of *Auckland Home Beautiful* which the agent showed me. So, your Number Twelve, Mr Messenger, so modern and light and full of colour, is going to be up there to be seen by everyone who comes into our new house. Isn't that wonderful.

It wasn't a question.

I just love the way you contrast the trees and the buildings, she went on. The juxtaposition is simply marvellous. Two completely different palettes, styles and techniques and moods. To me, it'll be like having two paintings.

I was somewhat enchanted by this young Trish Lallemand. It wasn't a romantic enchantment, love-at-first-sight or anything like that. But she did remind me so much of Fiona. No Scottish accent, of course, and much younger than my Fi, but with the same bubbling-over enthusiasm and love of life and art. I guessed she was one of those lucky people whose glass is always half-full (as they say), who is always excited — thrilled even — by novelty and beauty, which she manages to see everywhere she looks and in everyone she meets.

Number Twelve, she said, presenting it with an outstretched arm and an open palm. It's my favourite. I wanted it as soon as I saw it.

And so, as a result of her enthusiasm and my enchantment, I was pleased — for her — that she was to be Number Twelve's owner. And I said so, wanting to confide in her then the matter of the missing signature. Its absence had evidently gone unnoticed by everyone, so far, anyway, and knowing her I guessed she would treat the information as privileged 'insider knowledge'.

I was about to tell her — she was standing on one side of Number Twelve, I was on the other — when, suddenly, there was a man standing between us. It felt like a rude intrusion, and I was definitely offended, until Trish said brightly: Oh, David, there you are.

17.

IT WAS MR Lallemand, David Lallemand, the missing husband.

This is Mr Messenger, she said, indicating around her husband to me, who was, by now, staring at his wide back. He turned around at that, looked me up and down, somewhat grimly and critically I thought, evidently not approving of what he saw, and we shook hands uncordially, without speaking.

This is it, David, said Trish, indicating Number Twelve hanging on the wall in front of the three of us. Isn't it wonderful.

David Lallemand bent back slightly, his head to one side, looking out of the corner of his eyes as if bringing Number Twelve into focus for a better study.

This? he asked, glancing briefly at his wife for confirmation before returning his critical attention to the painting.

Yes, said Trish, apparently not noticing his implicit disapproval as I so easily had. Isn't it just perfect for the house.

At that, David Lallemand turned to me and said bluntly, There's something missing.

Oh, I know, I said quickly. But—

At that, he turned to Trish, who was now looking worried and dismayed. I don't like it, he said. I don't want to pay for it, Trish. I really don't.

He turned to me then. Look, Mr Messenger, he said, not rudely but coldly all the same. I don't know anything about you or art. I'm a businessman. Finance. Banking. All that. Haven't got a creative bone in my body. Usually I trust my wife's taste in these things. Absolutely. But, generally, I know what I like and, no offence, but I just don't like your painting.

Actually, I didn't care whether he liked it or not but I *did* care about Mrs Lallemand who was clearly confused and hurt. She looked at me with a puzzled and apologetic expression before looking up again at her husband and asking the obvious: David, but why?

Because, he said vehemently, something's missing.

I wanted to interrupt and explain but I was too slow. I was beaten by Mrs Lallemand who quickly asked the obvious: David, what?

I could see she was genuinely puzzled. I desperately wanted to reassure him about the missing signature, that I could easily add it, that I would, but I could see that this was about more than just a missing signature; this was a husband-wife argument about something else in which a third party would not be welcome. I felt embarrassed and sorry for the wife, and puzzled by the husband, and just wanted to walk away.

But suddenly the husband grabbed my elbow and forcibly turned me to face my Number Twelve.

This, he said pointing to trees in the foreground in front of the buildings, is Victoria Park, right?

Well, actually, I began to say, meaning to explain that my paintings are not meant to be realistic landscapes, but was interrupted by Mr Lallemand who was still gripping my elbow.

And here, he added, waving his somewhat pink and podgy hand over the buildings represented in the background, behind the trees, there is something missing.

What, David? asked his wife again, pleadingly. What on earth are you talking about?

She looked increasingly embarrassed.

Lallemand released my elbow then and turned to his wife. Can't you see? he asked.

No, David, I can't.

Well, there, right there — he pointed to the very middle of my Number Twelve — is where the Lallemand Tower should be. Turning to me again, he said, Completely missing. Can you even imagine what that's like for me? Missing.

And then, turning back to his wife, he continued. He purposely left out the Lallemand Tower, Trish. It's an insult. My new building. A monument to my success. How the hell can I be expected to pay for this painting and hang it in my house for all to see when it obviously doesn't even show my own building. It should be there, Trish, right... there.

At which he started repeatedly poking the hanging canvas.

Please don't do that, begged his wife.

He looked squarely at me then as if daring me to say something.

I knew, in fact, that he was both right and wrong. He was wrong about the location: the thick forest of plane trees in the foreground of Number Twelve, just beginning to shrivel, their living greenness fading to nature's beautiful but dying autumn colours, was painted from one of the many images of trees, bushes, shrubs, forests and flowers I have stored in my mental library. But he was sort of right that I had used a block of buildings near Victoria Park, but only as a model to communicate. I had no desire to reproduce the buildings accurately, with photographic realism; if I had omitted to show his beloved building it must have been a sub-conscious decision. I didn't remember his building — I still don't — but I can only assume that for some unremembered reason it didn't support what I was trying to convey.

In response to his unspoken demand for an explanation I simply shrugged and said, It's not meant to be realistic.

What!

He sounded insulted.

If you want an accurate portrait of your building, Mr Lallemand, I said, I suggest you engage a professional photographer.

I'm outa here, he said angrily. He reached forward then and peeled away the little red sticker from the wall, immediately adjacent to where I should have signed Number Twelve, screwed it up and dropped it on the floor. Come on, Trish, we're going.

His poor wife looked at me, turned, and continued to look back at me as she left, pulled along, trotting, by her angry husband, her expensive handbag bouncing against her hip, with an open-mouthed look of horror and shame, as if begging for forgiveness.

Mrs Barkstone, standing to one side but watching and listening, came to me at once, shaking her head.

That poor woman, she said. She really and truly loved your work. She was the first one here — waiting for me to open the room — and chose your Number Twelve at once. Without hesitation.

Zelnick, who never misses anything that happens in his domain, and whose eccentric style, strange syntax and indeterminate accent are all, I think, consciously assumed or exaggerated for effect, also appeared. He had a little red sticker attached to the end of his right index finger. He waved it in my face smugly, silent for a moment, before speaking.

Never mind, my friend, he said. I have list of many buyers waiting to buy this beautiful — but unsigned — Number Twelve.

With that, he theatrically pressed the new red sticker to the wall to replace the one which Mr Lallemand had removed and which now lay, crumpled, at my feet.

Stepping back, he stared smilingly down at the new sticker — not at all at the painting — his arms folded smugly. He turned to me then and said, Is sold already to Mr Burleigh-Brown, a name which meant nothing to me but made Mrs Barkstone smile and nod with approval and evident satisfaction.

I've never liked that Mr Lallemand, she said.

I don't suppose I'll ever see Mr Lallemand again although I still feel sorry for his wife. Indeed, Mrs Barkstone assured me that the lady is a serious and respected collector and that her wealthy husband, who proudly parades his ignorance of the arts, has always, until this evening, deferred to her superior knowledge, assuming that what his wife sees as a fine painting for her must therefore be a fine investment for him.

I could go and find the Lallemand Tower, wherever it is, but I won't.

It was a successful night in many ways, especially for me and Zelnick — if not for Mrs Lallemand — and evidently twelve satisfied buyers, so I wish I could say that that was how the day ended.

But I can't.

18.

I DIDN'T GET a taxi home; Zelnick insisted that his Bentley was at my disposal and that I would be driven home by his nephew.

He'll take you home for celebrating a good night, Zelnick had said.

I wanted to see Uncle Frank before I went home, so I directed my driver to Williamson Avenue. I'd turned off my phone while I was at the gallery. I turned it on, sitting in the car, and it came to life at once. There was a message from Uncle Frank's night matron, Jo-Anne.

Please call me back as soon as you can, she said.

I did as she asked. She answered at once, introduced herself and basically said she was so sorry but Uncle Frank had passed away peacefully earlier in the evening.

At exactly ten past eight, she said. We have to record the time of death, you understand.

Ten past eight. I was probably talking to — or rather listening to — that dreadful Mr Lallemand.

Believe me, Mr Messenger, your uncle's passing was utterly peaceful and painless. The ideal way to go for a man of his age and condition.

So, what do I have to do?

She said there was nothing for me to do. Not tonight, anyway. We're waiting for Doctor Goldson, she said. A formality. May I suggest you pop in tomorrow morning and see Yvonne. She'll know all about it. What to do and that. You'll need to collect his things, sign some papers, arrange a funeral director, that sort of thing. Tomorrow morning will be best. After a good night's sleep. Refreshed sort of thing.

So, that's what I have to take care of tomorrow morning. And then what?

Suddenly I feel tired, exhausted, and utterly alone. There's now no one in the world who cares for me or for whom I care. Sad as it was for Uncle Frank — dying alone, locked in his room, drugged and utterly unaware — I could see that it was also a release for him from his pain and confusion. And sad as it was for me — to be alone in this country in which I still feel somewhat strange — I could see that it was a release for me, too.

Indeed, it's been a big day in so many ways. A day of highs and lows.

I've got no more ties in London; everything's settled and the money's all in the bank. With Uncle Frank gone, I've got no more ties in Auckland. That means I'm finally free to say goodbye to Gregan and this flat. I'll buy a car and move at last to my little Saint Clair cottage in Bedford Street where — with Jaws for company — I'll be free of all obligations, free to shut out the world and paint whatever I want knowing that, whatever it is, Zelnick will sell it. Or not.

And if and when I stop painting, or if my paintings stop selling — I could easily go out of fashion or something — or if I get ill and can't paint, then I know Willy will continue to look after my money, just as he'll continue to look after Father's trust until, eventually, my dear mother's charities will be a few million dollars richer and the New Zealand Messenger line will come to an end.

But that's for the future. Meanwhile I have a fair bit to do. I'll have to clean out the studio and start packing. I'll start tomorrow after I've seen to Uncle Frank's affairs. I suppose I'll have to arrange a small funeral for him. I wonder who on earth will be there. Just as I wonder, when the time comes, who on earth will be at mine.

The Artist as an Old Man (Self-Portrait)

— THE END —